Love Remains

"Grief From Life, Grief From Loss"

My Journey from Loss (Bailey) to Found (Bettye)

Bettye Nicole

CONTENTS

DEDICATION LETTER

To my Lord and Savior Jesus Christ, I often try and find words to describe how grateful I am for who you are to me. You have been the one and only constant in my life! When I was disobedient, you loved me. When I rebelled, you loved me. When I turned my back on your commands, you loved me. When I didn't love myself, you never stopped loving me. Tears fill my heart and eyes when I think of the mercy and grace you have shown me throughout my life. I can never repay you but my hope is to devote every day of my life unto you and your work. I am forever your servant.

To my Bailey Nicole, you are and will forever be my greatest and best memory. I miss you beyond words. I do. It is because of you that I understand life and the brevity of it. I am so confident in God and His final rule that I no longer wish that you were here. My only hope is that I get to see you again. I know that I will. I will love you for eternity and a day. Though my heart aches, it's no longer a bad ache but one that creates this relentless devotion to God and His plan. It's an ache that pushes me to trust God, no matter what. Bailey, you were everything I could have ever prayed for and your gentle spirit, sweet smile and dimples shine through my heart daily. I will forever miss you.

To my three children on earth, you guys mean more to me than words can adequately describe. I love you guys so much and I am grateful for each moment that I get to spend on this side with you. I see so much potential in you guys. My prayer has and will forever be that you understand that God has a great plan for each of you. You all are the reason for many of my decisions and I pray that as you grow older that you understand the love that I have for you all but more importantly the love of God. I promise to be that Godly example and I promise to always be that mommy that you can count on until Christ take us all home.

To my mother, you are the sweetest, most caring person on earth. I love you more than you will ever know. Thank you for bringing me up in the fear and reverence of God. Thank you for staying on the phone with me for hours when I wanted to give up. Thank you for always giving me sound, godly wisdom and advice. Thank you for speaking to my heart and uplifting me when I was completely broken. I know that God handpicked you especially for me and I know that I would not be the woman that I am if it was not for you and your many sacrifices. You are my (S)hero.

To my siblings, I love you guys so much. I am so grateful for our closeness and only God could have stitched our bond together tightly. We have laughed, cried, fussed and laughed some more. You guys will never understand how much you mean to me and I love you all to the moon and back.

To my nieces and nephews, continue to strive for God's best. No matter how many times you fall in life, know that God is right there ready and willing to pick you up.

To my Bailey's Dash supporters, never in a million years would I had have imagined that God would use the pain of my grief to speak to the hearts of millions. God has a way to reach the hearts of the broken and oftentimes, it's through our own broken hearts. The Lord allowed a life altering pain, to break me. Then He allowed you guys to follow this journey from shattered to whole. I know that this was never truly about me. It was about God getting His glory and using this pain as a testament that He can and will walk with you through your grief (from life and loss). Thank you all for all the kind words, gifts and prayers that you have given over the last few years. I count you all as family. I love you guys!

To my editor Terrenique (Ipromise Media), I will forever be grateful to God for connecting us. I prayed for someone to help me with this project and I believe wholeheartedly God answered my request in you. You pushed me to "dig deeper" and share my truth. Thank you for being encouraging and believing in this book and my testimony. You are truly the best!

Special thanks to my Angel Sisters **Jameelah Davis, Tamira Dunn, London Labriola, Erica McAfee, Jewel Carey-Smith** and **Qiana Wright** for being such a blessing in my life. We met under the worst circumstances ever (loss) but I know that God divinely orchestrated our sisterhood. Our love for our babies and to see other angel moms healed is the stitch that has bonded us forever.
I love you ladies to life!

Erica Hearns (Formatter) **Rachel Arterberry** (Editor) and **Montel Moore** (Sound Engineer) thank you guys for using your gift to help get this project complete. You guys were an answer to my prayers. You guys rock!

FOREWORD

Perhaps you've read the title of this book and thought, "it looks great and it seems very compelling" and then perhaps you wondered, "who is Bettye Nicole?" Bettye is my friend, and a confidant to many. Bettye is Bailey's mommy, she is Alasijah, Darius Jr. and Briyah's mommy too. She is a godly woman, a faithful servant and a purposed leader. I know all of these things because over the last couple of years, I've been received into her life; both her grief life and her healing life. The day we first "met" was on social media. My chance encounter with Bettye came from a seed that God planted long ago, He uniquely crafted Bettye's story and ordered her steps way before her existence.

Our day to meet had come. Bettye made a video in honor of Bailey, her four months and two-day old daughter who had recently gone home to be with Jesus. That heartrending video garnered millions of views and I was but one in a million that viewed it. Immediately, I was filled with sadness like many others. For her pain, she was receiving the most poignant condolences from people all around the world. Certainly, not the way she ever hoped to gain stardom. The year had changed her, it began with her sharing photos of her pregnant tummy, then welcoming her daughter into the world with pictures of her radiant smile and videos of her cooing. Who would have thought that by the end of the year a mother would be sharing a goodbye video and pictures from her daughter's funeral? To this video, I had a visceral reaction that was so provoking I sat and felt upset at the very one I trusted the most.

I sat in awe reading all of the love comments being sent to this grief-stricken mother. The majority of those people sending condolences had never even met her, including me. I reached out to Bettye because I heard God's voice that day so loudly, He told me to "say something." I questioned, "What does 'something' mean Father?" I didn't get a response. God had urged me like this before in similar situations. At times, it felt as if He was using me to reveal what He was saying to His people. The words never felt like my own.

The words God gave me were exactly what I was mandated to say to a mom who was at her lowest, most fearful and irreparable place. A woman and mother who was lost, in unfamiliar territory and couldn't find home. A lost mom looking for her loss, her precious daughter, the daughter she never fathomed a day without. It was as if I could hear Bettye calling out and I followed the sound of her screams. I found her but not without my own fear. How would she receive a stranger asking for her hand in the dark? I declared the truth, I knew that I was not alone and that God would not leave Bettye alone. God guided me and I followed. I wrote the words He asked of me. I expected nothing, instead, I only hoped that what I said might serve as a bit of light to help her along her way. What ignited in that message that day wasn't the smallness of a lantern's flame, but rather a holy campfire.

I wrote to Bettye what I would hope someone would write to me on my worst day. My worst day would be the death of a child. While I haven't personally experienced the death of any of my own children, I have experienced great loss of many kinds, including my own pregnancies and an infant I babysat as a teenager that was a victim of SIDS. I've experienced children drowning, murdered and called home by cancer. I've had the opportunity to speak with many mothers who've lost children over the years through my non-profit foundation. I am the Founder of The Happy Heart Foundation, a non-profit organization dedicated to fighting for children's rights to be freed from harm. We also offer grief support to parents of children who have died and ministry services relative to child mortality and putting hope back in children's hearts who are alive.

I've become passionate about understanding infant loss and how our Lord helps us to grieve and mend brokenness. I wrote to Bettye with the salt of the ocean dripping down my cheeks. I wanted to talk to her and walk with her as a friend and sister. I wanted her to know that a thousand miles away, there was a

mom who loved her and would be there to make sure that
Bailey was always remembered. But more importantly, for her
to know that I would endlessly be there as a comforter when
the days felt infinite and the ground ever trembling beneath
her. See, these words were not my own, instead it was a
message I was told to give to her. I meant every word, but I
was only the messenger.

I got my first response from Bettye after I sent the message
and instantly our souls found one another in a galaxy of stars.
Just two mom souls that kind of said, "Oh there you are, I've
been waiting for you." I figured that my purpose was to
mentor Bettye and relay the messages that God placed on my
heart to her, but Bettye turned out to be one of my very own
spiritual leaders. I often found myself asking "How does she
do it? How in the world does she have the energy to be there
for me when I need the support the most?". I discovered that
what she was doing for me and countless others who followed
her was the natural medicine that's only purpose was to heal.
Bettye was navigating the impenetrable terrain by helping
others and serving God's hurting people with unwavering
faith.

I stopped seeing her as a mom who lost a child. She wasn't
helpless, and what happened to her could not become her. It is
the system of the devil's propaganda to make sufferers more
hope-less and to deplete their hope-full. Bettye would not be
defined by her loss. Instead, she was a mom with a daughter in
heaven and she chased fireflies in the night to find her way.

Directionally, the way to Bailey was to walk in love with God. Until they meet again.

I have never met anyone like Bettye and I might never again. What I know is that there isn't a way out, only a way forward. Every hour of the day Bettye moved her burning feet one step ahead at a time, as pieces of skin were peeling back she chased the fireflies. With each motion ahead, I saw and heard Bettye declare, "fear is a liar!" Each delicate movement brought her to this moment. This book will captivate you and pull you to your knees because when YOU cannot stand, you KNEEL. Her persistence was simply bridging the gap between the pain and the fulfillment of God's promises.

Sincerely,

London Labriola

GRIEF FROM LIFE, GRIEF FROM LOSS

Grief is something I rarely had heard of until it unexpectedly came into my heart. Sorrow captured my every emotion, turning every good and positive emotion I've ever felt into pain. A pain so indescribable that no words could ever be sufficient. Grief changes you. Grief changed me. It transforms the make-up of your heart, alters your thoughts and changes your very outlook on life.

I thought on ways to describe how my heart felt when Bailey didn't wake up. Yet every word, every sentence, every paragraph only explained a surface feeling of the pain. There were no words that could describe the stabbing ache that I felt in my heart and in my mind. Our hearts are located internally and are woven together with our soul and emotions. Bailey's death brought on both physical and physiological pain; pain that reached into the depth of a place that I had no idea existed. "How would I ever recover? Where would I find hope? How could these shattered pieces of my heart ever be mended?" Grief exposes hidden pain that you may have experienced as early as your childhood and all the other past events that you've never fully healed from. Grief sheds light on the events and pain that you swept under the rug in your heart, hiding it from yourself, your offenders, loved ones and most importantly, your future. As you walk through this journey with me you will understand that in order to experience true healing, you must not only deal with the *grief from loss* but also the *grief of life*. It is true that God is working all things together for the good of those who love Him to those who are called according to His purpose. -*Romans 8:28 (ESV)*

Chapter 1

DOLL HOUSE DREAMS

As a young girl, I always dreamed of having a family. Like most young girls, I wanted a family that consisted of both mother and father, happily married, living and serving God. I would request a doll house, family van and dog almost every Christmas for several years. I lived vicariously through this little doll house family. I imagined myself as a Godly wife whose husband loved God, her and his children dearly. I imagined them never arguing and the kids never feeling rejected and alone. As I pushed that little van, I prayed and hoped in my little heart that this would someday be my reality; that someday I would have a Christian, functional family that was filled with love and stability. I grew up not knowing my biological father. Often times I daydreamed about what life would be like if he was around. I don't particularly remember a moment where I felt the rejection of not knowing him until I got older. I think it's safe to say that my household was dysfunctional. I had the most loving, Christ-like, sweetest, soft spoken mother in the world, but my stepfather on the other hand was different. My stepfather had an alcohol addiction. We watched as he drank his life away and as a result, we suffered severely from verbal abuse. Every payday was the same. He would leave for weeks at a time and then come home whenever his check was gone. I hated this for my mother. More than anything I hated this for him. I could tell that he wanted to do better some days, but he was bound by his addiction. Through it all I developed a greater love and appreciation for my mom. She taught me at an early age what it meant to truly love another human. Selflessly, my mom tolerated his addiction for years. I prayed long and hard for my mom to leave him, but my prayers always seemed to go unanswered. From an early age, I sensed that our family was dysfunctional, nonetheless I still learned valuable lessons on love, endurance, and long suffering. Despite the adversity we faced, I am still very grateful for my upbringing and the life lessons that I learned. I love my stepfather with all my heart and still to this day I pray daily for his deliverance. Also, both of my mother's parents passed away at an early age so I didn't get a chance to meet her mom or father. Having no living grandparents affected me as well. What I wouldn't give to have had spent just one day with them.

Around the age of fifteen, I began to inquire about my father's whereabouts. I wanted to meet him so badly. I was receiving a social security check from him and at the time I had no clue that he was sick. My mom was very vague about my father, keeping all conversations regarding him to a minimum. I believe that she was trying to protect me. I pleaded with her daily to search for him. She would sometimes pretend to be on the phone with him, but nothing ever came out of it. No weekend visits, phone calls or text messages. Finally, one day after my plea, she gave me his mother's number. My heart was beating at high speed as I thought on what to say when my dad's mom picked up. I lived all these years without knowing them and now this was my chance. I prayed that they would accept me.

My plan was to call my dad's mother the same day I got her number, but my anxiety got the best of me. I practiced my lines for hours in the mirror. I wanted to be sure that I said the right thing. I remember my stomach shifting uneasily as I pressed the numbers and within the first ring I hung up. After a few pep talks, I finally built up the nerve to call again. I didn't know what to expect but at this point I didn't care. I had to do it. The conversation started off great. She was so happy to hear from me and she shared almost everything that came to her mind about my father and how much she loved him. She mentioned how he traveled and loved music. I was soaking up every piece of information that she shared because he was a part of me, a part that I had yet to meet. The more she spoke, the more I imagined what he was like. I listened in and waited patiently for her to share his current location. All the while thinking, I can't believe this is happening. I was so happy that I couldn't sit down, I leaned against the wall and just smiled. I watched as my mom frantically cleaned the kitchen. I figured she was just as nervous as I was. I finally asked my Grandma, "where is he?" I had no idea I would receive the news that I did. Honestly, I was not prepared as she whispered, "Oh your father is dead, he passed away". "What, he's dead?" I tried to stay calm for the remainder of the conversation but that wall that I leaned in on happily at first, became my support. When I hung up, I screamed and cried. Punching myself and hating that I did not call sooner. You see, she shared that my father had cancer and he died just a few months before I called her. She said that they searched for me but were not able to find me. Those words "We searched and searched but could not find you" still pierce my heart today. I was angry at my mom but angrier at myself. "Why didn't I think to call sooner?" During that call, I found out that I had a brother as well. Still to this day, I have yet to meet him. I pray often that God allows us to cross paths, only if it is in His will.

My father's death devastated me. I had so many questions, so many experiences I wanted to share with him, but he was gone. I wish I had sought counseling or knew the importance of seeking God for healing, but instead, I swept all of my hurt and emotions under the rug in my heart.

The pain I encountered left me vulnerable. I was stuck trying to fit in and fill a void that only God could fill. My eager desire to fit in led me to even more hurt. I had a brother that didn't like me very much at the time. He picked on me for years. I vividly remember one day he hit me in my head with a baseball bat. He had no remorse and claimed that it wasn't intentional, but I knew that it was. I was so desperate at times to make amends with him that I was willing to put myself in a vulnerable place, only for him to turn and be upset with me shortly after. It was weird. I never understood what caused him to treat me that way, but I believe that he felt like our mom showed me favoritism. That was not the case. There were seven of us plus three (adopted siblings) and my mom loved us all the same. It was something in his own heart. Something that I will probably never fully understand. Our relationship is okay now, thank God.

A few months later, I joined the church that my brother attended. The members of the church were adamant about getting to know God, studying His word and spending time in prayer. During that season, I began to build my relationship with the Lord and He was my focal point. I brought Jesus to my household and every day at noon, I made my sisters pray and cry out to God. I've caught them a few times running away from me when the clock struck twelve. They wanted to play like kids, but I wanted them to learn the importance and power of prayer. I felt like it was my responsibility as their older sister to teach them. I was still friends with folks that pushed me toward sin and not Christ. As a result, I slowly began to drift away from God. The season of following Christ didn't last long because I wanted to fit in so badly within my environment. I strongly believe that He used this time so that I can look back on my low days and remember what I truly had in Him: relationship and consistency. Soon, my church attendance, Bible and prayer time began to decrease and suddenly, my desires changed.

I started to pursue an earthly relationship like never before. I wanted to feel loved. I wanted to experience companionship like I saw on television. I ignored both warnings from my mom and the Lord because I wanted to do things my own way. I always dreamed of being with a godly man but where we lived and the condition of my heart at this point, I was not willing to wait. My thinking shifted, I started hanging out with folks from the hood and soon after I desired a hood guy.

I was sixteen when I met Greg and by the age of twenty I had two children. I was living on my own in public housing and working dead end jobs just to survive. I managed to get my GED and I was grateful to have my own little family. Although it was dysfunctional as well, dysfunction was all I knew. I married at the age of twenty-one and by the age of twenty-five I had three children. My life was the absolute opposite of my doll house dream. It was more like a nightmare.

I will say this, everything wasn't all bad all the time, *but* it is embarrassing to think on the choices that I made during that time. I knew better. I knew that God had a better plan but like most women, I figured if I did things my own way and prayed every now and again, God would still bless me and my union. I was brainwashed into thinking that once I prayed hard enough and loved strong enough, things would eventually get better. I was living in an environment that bred dysfunction. I was introduced to different dysfunctional behaviors that could have led to me losing my life. I was chasing after Greg and the life he lived. Later in life, I began to dream of that lifestyle chasing me. During this time of (spiritual) reckless living, my seventeen-year-old sister was the victim of a drive by shooting that left her paralyzed. She began dating her guy shortly after I met Greg and we were both dangerously in love and willing to forsake everything we knew that was right and true to be with them. That day four of my girlfriends, my sister and I were headed to the hood to hang with our guys. I was driving a Monte Carlo, so three of us were in the front and three in the back. As we headed that way I felt this feeling in the pit of my stomach that was warning me not to go. I didn't want to share this with them because even I couldn't explain the *why*. So, I circled around town taking all kind of detours. Finally, I could no longer resist their request, so I ignored that feeling and went. Not even five minutes of parking, we were running for our lives as bullets flew past me and under my foot. I ran into a neighbor's house and moments later I heard the screams, "Elgina is shot". I ran in the bathroom and dropped to my knees in despair. I called my mom with the little breath that I had left and told her, and I listened as she cried and yelled hysterically. As the weeks passed and I watched as she lay in bed with tubes in her frail body, I hated making that decision to drive out there. It grieved me deeply, but I hid it from everyone. Talk about a devastating, life altering event. This was it. She was with me,

I was supposed to protect her. I taunted myself and the fact that I knew I shouldn't have went out there pierced my conscience daily. I thought about if I had continued in God's way and not run away from my relationship with Him maybe this would have never happened. I didn't realize I carried the grief of that night in my heart for years. Other events occurred throughout the years, but I plan to share that in another book.

> *An analogy I like to use for that period of my life is this. I imagine a puzzle of my life, put together. Several pieces are missing already, my biological father, Grandmother and Grandfather now there are several other pieces that are bent and torn badly. This sums up my life up into this point*

I admonish you to wait on the Lord and follow His ways. Every decision that you make comes with its share of consequences and the sting of some of those consequences will follow us for the rest of our lives. God's way is the best way. Don't connect yourself with just anyone, allow the Lord to guide your path and make your connections. Submit this area to Him. He'll provide you with friends, business partners and relationships that are built on purpose not convenience.

You may be in a place where you have friends or acquaintances that you know are toxic but you refuse to let them go. You may have received warning after warning but you ignore them because you don't want to offend or ruffle some feathers. God did His part. He sent the signs you prayed for, but you're blatantly ignoring them. God never allows us to walk into any situation unwarned, He loves us too much. Just as a parent put safety guards around the house to protect their small infant from getting hurt, God does the same thing for us. He places safeguards in His word to keep us from experiencing unnecessary hurt.

Be assured and know that when you make mistakes and follow the wrong path, God's grace will lead us back to His perfect will. If you have experienced hurt and pain from your family or even in relationships, seek healing. When you are whole, you make better decisions. Allow God to heal those wounds from your past. It is necessary for your future.

Chapter 2

LOVE ON TOP, PAIN AT THE BOTTOM

In 2011, after years of living according to my own will and desires, I slowly began to transition back into church. February of that year (my birthday) Greg and I were leaving a club when I said something that really upset him. We were both drunk and before I knew it, he pressed his foot on the gas, I mean pedal to the metal. I yelled "Please slow down", but it was too late. We were speeding straight into the side of a brick house. The only thing I heard was a loud "Boom". I remember calling my mom telling her that I was bleeding a lot and I needed her prayers because I didn't think that I would make it. I was intoxicated yet the fear of the Lord overtook me. I knew that I wasn't ready to see Jesus, so I begged him for another chance, my soul was at stake. I had been gambling with my life for far too long and I knew what God required of me. I wasn't ready to meet Him.

Thank God, I only suffered a broken nose and because I was drunk, I said I saw more blood than I really did. The doctors told my mom that they couldn't believe I didn't suffer more and that my seat belt saved my life. Deep in my thoughts, I knew it was God that spared me. I vowed that day to never drink again. Years passed, and I stayed the course, following after Jesus. It was a Tuesday night in June of 2014. I went to Bible study and left feeling so refreshed and renewed, I felt that God was up to something big in my life. That night, I came home and joked around with Greg before heading to bed. He was up and his eyes were glued to his cellphone, as usual.

As I prepared to go to sleep, I kneeled on the side of the bed and said a quick prayer. I thanked the Lord for everything that He was doing in my life and all the things He planned to do. I said, "Lord if there is anything you would like for me to know, please show me." I literally prayed that prayer not expecting to receive an answer so quickly. Boy, was I in for a heart-wrenching, life changing revelation. The next morning came and as I was preparing for work, Greg's phone was on the edge of the bed. Usually he keeps his phone locked and stored away while he's asleep. I stared over at the phone and thought to myself, "nope I'm not going to check his phone". But there was this tugging in my spirit, a tugging that I knew came from God. So, I picked up his phone and went into the bathroom. I was literally trembling because I knew whatever it was God was about to show me would break my heart. I had found myself in this predicament time and time again but this time it just felt different. I sat on the bathroom floor and clicked into the messages, in complete disbelief, my heart dropped. I stepped out of the bathroom and threw his phone on the bed. At that moment, it felt like I was tossing aside my family, my heart, and my life. As he jumped up to catch his phone he also caught the responsibility of ruining our family. I could not believe he was having another affair. Though my heart and mind were shattered, I made it through this day at work and home but it was tough.

The following day, I counted the days since I had my last menstrual. I had a strong feeling that I was pregnant, but I needed confirmation. I met with one of my gal-pals who worked at a pregnancy clinic and she gave me a home test. To no surprise, two solid lines appeared on the screen. I was pregnant and in a matter of days, my life had been turned upside down. I held this secret for almost a month and I refused to tell Greg because I didn't want him to stay with me just because of the pregnancy. A big part of me wished that I wasn't pregnant, while another part of me knew that this was God's plan. Despite it all, we agreed to work things out. I still had hope that this pregnancy would change him.

Weeks later, I discovered that he and the young lady were still involved with each other. It was then that I called my mom in a heart-broken rage. "Momma I am pregnant and Greg is leaving me." I was on the side of the road, crying my heart out. I hacked into his email and read some messages that they had exchanged and I couldn't believe all of this was happening. I believe that grief had already set into my heart. Although we were still in the same household and lying in the same bed every night, this affair and the grief of it all was wrecking me. I had held on to hope for years but deep down, I knew that God was not up to what I thought that He was but instead was shifting things in my heart and mind in preparation.

Nights were long and cold during my entire pregnancy. I cried an awful lot. I thought to myself "What is going on in heaven? Why would God allow me to go through this again? How could I ever leave now? How?" Here I am thirty years old with three children and one on the way. Who would ever want to re-marry me?" These were some of the many thoughts that ran through my mind. I didn't think highly of myself. I just didn't. So, I stayed. I endured the verbal and physical abuse, the affairs, the lies and everything else because it was easier. It was so tough for me knowing what I knew while maintaining the smile of a person that appeared to be happy. Very few people knew of this truth. I preferred to keep it that way.

Around my twelfth week, I thought that my pregnancy wouldn't make it because I had a small hemorrhage near my placenta. I prayed and after a few ultrasounds for precaution I was in the clear. I didn't have any more complications or any other scary moments so I was very grateful for that.

I have learned that no one wants to go through tough times, yet it is the tough times that build our character, endurance, and our faith. Many people would have just simply left the situation but for me, it wasn't that easy. When I love, I love hard and it's hard for me to turn off that button. I watched my mom stay and tried to work on her relationship, and this helped influence my decision. Every lie and broken promise, every punch and kick led me to think of how important it was to endure and fight for my relationship. I couldn't give up. On the other hand, with every lie and broken promise, I would say surely this is it, I am leaving. A few days would pass and there was no communication, then I gave in and I fell back into the same trap of trying to make things right. Don't get me wrong, I was not perfect. I was so broken emotionally that I nagged him to death. I didn't believe anything that he said and my insecurities only made matters worse. But I had a change of heart and I longed for deliverance and just to be happy, but my comfortability said, 'just be patient, things will get better'. Things never did. Things got worse. As I mentioned earlier, dysfunction breeds dysfunction. God allowed this situation to build me up. I needed to experience pain and learn a deeper lesson. I believe that this pain shaped and prepared me for what was to come with Bailey.

BAILEY NICOLE

I started searching for a name once the doctor "convinced" me that I was having a girl. You see, six weeks into my pregnancy I believed that I was having a baby boy. I didn't have the symptoms that I had with my girls plus I believed that if God allowed this seed to be birthed in me, surely it would be a baby boy. I prayed for a baby boy many years ago, and I didn't want a girl this time around. From my experience, I learned that boys were much easier. I had already picked out his name, "Kingston". In every conversation, I referred to my bump as "him". When I found out that he was a she, it was another blow to my heart. After all I had endured I thought the Lord would grant my request and give me what my heart truly longed for. He didn't. Looking back, I understand why. God always has a greater plan and purpose, He is strategic in all that He does and His plan was for me to give birth to a beautiful baby girl. I named her Bailey, Bailey Nicole.

BAILEYS BABY SHOWER

January 25[th,] 2015, my sister in love and one of my best gal pals gave me the best baby shower ever. I mean, they decked the place out with ladybugs. I was so grateful for all the support everyone had shown me but deep down inside I was a broken mess. On the surface, I was full of Joy. I smiled and interacted with everyone hoping that my brokenness didn't show in my countenance. That day Bailey received tons of gifts. I didn't have to purchase anything but a car seat and a diaper bag. I was overwhelmed with gratitude. God was showering me with His love and although I didn't fully feel it at the time, I knew that God was with me. This was also the beginning of my love for ladybugs.

LABOR AND DELIVERY

The last few weeks of my pregnancy were tough. I was

having bad lower back pain because of how Bailey was positioned. It got so bad that I was taking prescribed pain medicine just to get to a comfortable space. Every day after the thirty-seventh week I prayed that she would come, I just wanted to be comfortable again.

During my final doctor's appointment, my doctor stripped my membranes. I've had this procedure done before with two of my other children so I knew that I would go into labor that day. For some reason, I have quick labors. I went to the Goodwill to search for some last-minute gems and while I was there the contractions started. As the contractions got more intense, I couldn't help but think about how my life was about to change.

I prayed that things would get better in my marriage and that Bailey's arrival would somehow mend our broken family back together. I kept track of my contractions for the next few hours and before you know it, I was officially in labor. We packed the kids in the car and we were on our way. I started to panic because the hospital where Bailey was scheduled to be delivered was in Illinois and I was in St. Louis. That's about a twenty to twenty-five-mile difference. We went to the first hospital and upon arrival I knew that I was very close to delivering. Once we made it inside, I was informed that the hospital's triage was full. The nurses told me it would be at least thirty minutes before they would be able to examine me. My contractions were less than five minutes apart so we left. We drove about thirteen more miles to the next hospital. This wasn't the best plan knowing that I was so close but we were running out of options, so I had to make the decision quickly. Once we arrived, they wheeled me right down the hall. As I changed my clothes, I felt the pain intensifying. Labor pains are tough and with every contraction the pain literally took my breath and thoughts away. While headed there, I was thinking of life; while contracting I pondered if I was near death. The pain was excruciating. Within twenty minutes Bailey Nicole had made her entrance into the world. The labor progressed rapidly and there wasn't even a doctor present. A nurse literally had to catch Bailey. She weighed in at eight pounds.

> *This was significant because the number eight means new beginnings in biblical numerology.*

Bailey was beautiful, and she was everything that I could have imagined and more. She had these deep dimples and this dark black hair that was perfect. As I laid looking at her, I was reminded of this scripture in John:

> *When a woman is giving birth, she has sorrow because her hour has come, but when she has delivered the baby, she no longer remembers the anguish, for joy that a human being has been born into the world. John 16:21 ESV*

I had joy. Although I had travailed and gave birth to Bailey, the challenges in other parts of my life continued on.

As I reflect on that day I realize that her birth and death had a lot in common. They were both quick and unexpected. Quick and unexpectedly she came into the world. Quick and unexpectedly is how she left this world.

BAILEY IS HERE

The first time I held her in my arms all I could do was stare into her full eyes. She was the biggest baby I've ever delivered, with a sweet and gentle spirit. I was in love all over again and that day I understood why God allowed me to give birth to such a blessing. I needed her, I needed to feel that dependency from her. I had three older children but they didn't need me like she did. The very first night that I delivered her, Greg left me at the hospital to go skating. I was so down but instead of looking at what he did, I poured all my heart into my new bundle of joy. I flashed back to every moment of rejection that I felt in my heart, but the Lord gave me a feeling of belonging through her. The first two days with Bailey were a breeze. I received so many compliments on how beautiful she was and how she was so well behaved. The doctors and nurses could not believe how much hair she had. I tried to breastfeed her but it didn't work as I planned, so we switched to baby formula. Later, I regretted switching to the formula because it caused constipation which caused her to fuss.

I was discharged from the hospital on my birthday, February 26th, 2015. I was so grateful to be home with my children and our newest little blessing. I didn't want anything from anyone. My only prayer was that God would restore my peace and He did.

I stayed home with Bailey for about two weeks before I had to return to school. I was finishing up my last semester so I was required to be present if not all, most of the time so that I could graduate and get my degree on time. I couldn't stand leaving my baby at home. I called two million times just to see what she was doing. Greg took Bailey to all her doctor's visits and often times he would call me while he was there or record the conversations between him and the doctor. Although Bailey never had any serious health issues, I still wanted to make sure that there wasn't any signs or symptoms that I missed. Approximately two months after returning to school, I returned to work. I was so excited to see my co-workers and they were happy to finally see me and to see me happy. My coworkers knew that I was down and discouraged when I first found out that I was pregnant. They also knew that I was going through things in my marriage. They supported me throughout it all.

ANNIVERSARY TRIP

May 25th, 2015 was our ten-year wedding anniversary. I planned a getaway trip for a week to California. It was my little gift to myself for successfully making it through college and of course, an anniversary treat for him. Although our marriage was in shambles, I was confident that a trip was something that we both really needed. My mom was upset that I was going with him and not my children. She felt as though they deserved it more than he did. His behavior hadn't changed and this grieved her heart. I wrestled with if we would take Bailey on the trip or leave her at home, we decided to let her stay with my brother and sister in love. We had an awesome time while on vacation and I was grateful for the time away but I missed my children, especially my sweet Bailey. The night we made it back in town, Greg was out the door and things went back to the way they were. Deep down in my heart I felt the disconnection; we were definitely drifting.

Each day of my life, as I knew it, involved some intense shifting and shaking. I dreamt about a better life but the thought of that life, without Greg was a hard pill to swallow. I also felt like if I didn't make a change, I would continue to lose myself. My emotions were constantly up and down; I longed for a consistent flow of joy and peace. I knew that I did not have that with him and deep down I knew that I never would. The fruit of the spirit comes from God and God alone but no one should consistently strip you of it. That is not God's plan.

> *But the fruit of the Spirit is love, joy, peace, forbearance,*
> *kindness, goodness, faithfulness, gentleness, and self-*
> *control. Against such things there is no law.*
> *Galatians 5:22-23*

Always remember to trust God, especially when He begins tugging on your heart to let certain things or relationships go. It is for a reason. Don't kick against change especially when you know that the Lord is orchestrating it. You may just be kicking against God.

Bailey Nicole

February 24, 2015-June 26, 2015

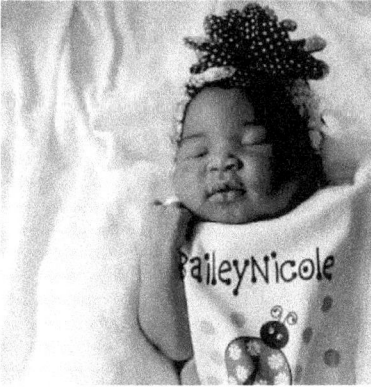

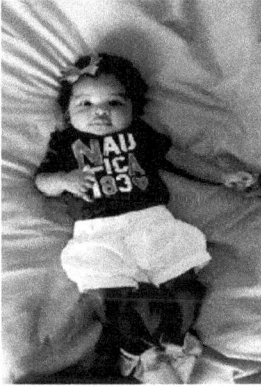

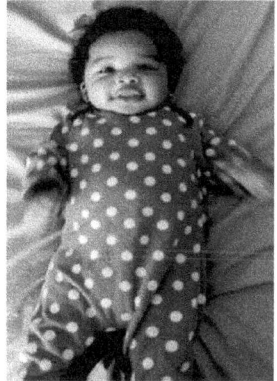

CHAPTER 3

LOSING BAILEY

June 25, 2015 was a day like any other day. I worked for a few hours then came home. Around 7pm that evening, I gave Bailey her bath and began to relax and prepare for my interview the following morning. My Mom and sister came by to visit us. I was so shocked that they braved the storm just to come over, yet very grateful. I needed to talk to my mom about some things that had been going on and I wanted to get her advice on what to do next.

Greg had shared with me that he was planning to go on a trip with his crew. I knew that the young lady he was having an affair with would go on the trip as well. We argued and argued about it and I was drained. That evening, nothing seemed out of the ordinary. Bailey was cheerful as usual and the kids were enjoying each other's company. Around 8:30pm, I made Bailey a bottle. My sister was holding her so I allowed her to feed her. But for some odd reason, she wouldn't eat. I thought nothing of it. Bailey was on a really good schedule. At

9pm, I usually set her down in her crib and she would fall asleep peacefully all by herself. As her bed time approached, she began to get a little cranky, so my sister placed her in her crib. Minutes later, as they were walking out the door to leave, I heard Bailey crying. I ran up the stairs to make sure she was ok and flicked on the lights as she looked up with a smile on her face. I said, "Bailey it's bed time". I gave her a pacifier and began to gently pat her on her back. After a minute or so, I crept back to the door, turned the light off and exited. That was the last time I saw Bailey alive, the very last time.

Looking back on that night, I believe that the Lord allowed me to see my baby one more time in her waking state. I got a final chance to see her smile. He knew full well the devastation I would face the next morning. I just wish that I knew.

Everyone had settled in for the night but I couldn't sleep. Major decisions flashed before me. I replayed the conversation with Greg and my Mom in my head. I was preparing my heart to walk away from my marriage if Greg decided to go on that trip. I knew that if I was going to have some sort of peace in that area, uncomfortable decisions would have to be made. I laid down, then sat back up. In the middle of the night, I scrolled back and forth through Facebook, then Instagram, read a few scriptures, shuffled from left to right, trying to find peace, but it was to no avail. As I listened to the storm, I began to talk to the Lord. What I said that night isn't something that I remember all too well, but I do know that I had a real heart to heart with God that night. I needed Him more than ever.

Finally, around 2 am, my brother sent a message in our family group chat. I was so ecstatic that someone else was up beside me. The first thing he asked was, "what are you doing up?" "I can't sleep", I replied. We went back and forth a few times and around 2:28am, I heard Greg come in the door. He locked the door and soon I drifted off to sleep.

I woke up the next morning feeling burdened, and heavy in my spirit. I had an interview that morning and the drive was about forty-five minutes long. It was storming outside but I was determined to drive through it just to make it on time. I walked over to my closet and I heard so clearly "check on Bailey".

I ignored it, "Bailey's ok" I thought. Her schedule was consistent, she usually woke up around 8am. After a few seconds, I thought maybe I should peep on her. I stepped away from my closet and walked toward her bed. I leaned in and rubbed her leg and it was stiff. Before breaking out in complete disbelief, I rubbed her back just to see if she would make any movements. She never moved. An unexplainable sense of dread and fright came over me. I leaned in and rubbed her leg and I felt stiffness again. Almost in a panicking state, I rubbed her back again. Her back was frozen solid and lifeless. Immediately, I cried, yelled and ran into the room to get Greg. I screamed for my baby. It was an agonizing, heart piercing scream that came from a place of unbelief and pain. "*How could the Lord allow this to happen to me, to my family, to my life?*" Greg rushed up the stairs to meet me and all I could say was "Bailey's not breathing. Omg, she's breathing. Lord no." I screamed.

I quickly grabbed my phone to call my Mom but she didn't answer. To this day, I don't know why 911 wasn't my first call but for me I knew that it was my mom who could help me not lose my mind. I heard Greg's agonizing cry from the other room. I tried dialing 911, my hands were shaking as I whispered, "Lord, no, please, Lord, please". The 911 dispatcher answered my call but it was hard for me to get the words out. She kept asking me these questions that seemed in the moment, irrelevant. I just needed her to breathe, I needed her to wake up and smile at me. I needed God to restore life back into her lifeless body. My mom called me back and I ended the call with 911 and just cried out to her. She was heading to work and she could hear the pain in my voice. I managed to tell her what happened and she yelled "I'm on my way". The 911 dispatcher called me back and began to explain to me how important it was for Greg to do chest compressions. But it was too late, I cried and said, "Greg did attempt CPR but he stopped". He picked her up and walked through the house holding our Bailey in his arms. Every room that he came in, I quickly ran out of. I couldn't bear the thought let alone the sight of my baby girl being propped in her father's arm, completely lifeless. The only glimpse I did get was him holding her up, her little fist was balled up. "Why me? Why her? Why now?" I cried. Minutes later, I heard the sirens and the doorbell rang, the ring that day was like a song. A song of dread. The first police officer bust in and asked, "Where is she?" I pointed upstairs. I would never forget the look of despair that was on his face. The officer bolted upstairs. Every bit of my strength that I once wore so proudly had left me completely. I felt like giving up, I didn't want to be strong, I didn't want to face this. I wanted my Bailey. I sat on the couch downstairs, my mom and step-father raced through the door and ran over to me. A weight, the size of a grain of sand lifted off me. Although that is extremely small, it helped.

The paramedics and police were still upstairs working on Bailey and conducting their investigation. The news spread like wild fire, "Bailey was gone." My family flocked at my house and with every knock at the door and ring of the doorbell, Bailey's death became more real. I secretly kept pinching myself. It all felt like a bad dream and I believed that at some point I'd wake up. More officers and investigators began to flood my home. My little neighborhood was packed with cops like a scene off of a crime show. I was interviewed by the officer in charge, he was very stern. We went over the details of the story twice. With every question, I grew more and more agitated. I just wanted to cry, that's all. No questions, no answers, just let me cry. The police officer scanned the room and noticed that I had Bible verses taped on the wall. He turned to me and asked, "Are you a Christian?" With tears in my eyes I shook my head and said "yes". He said, "So am I. I lost my daughter a few years ago and I know this is very tough for you right now but I know your faith will help you get through this. We did everything we could, but your daughter is gone."

Although I knew this already, when he said it, it pierced my soul. Mentally I left my body. Every word that he said from that moment on went through one ear and slipped out through the next. I just stared and shook my head as if I was listening.

It seemed as though the investigation took a life time. In my heart, I kept hoping that she would start breathing again or that they would yell "OMG it's a miracle!" I remember my mom being on the phone with the first lady of our then church, she handed me the phone. As I listened she said, "Go speak life over your baby". I was so upset that she would suggest such a thing that I threw the phone across the room. "Speak life? Death had already defeated her", I thought to myself. Death defeated me. Death defeated my family.

Reflecting on that call and her response caused me more pain in my latter stages of grief. If I had only had the faith that she had. If only I would have at least given it a try.

Every second of every minute that went by that day, I felt it. Within every hour it became more and more real to me. Bailey was in heaven and I would never ever see her again on this side of earth. Every time I thought about it I became more distant from my true self, from my other kids and my reality. Nothing would ever be the same.

FINAL MOMENTS

It is all the final moments about that day and as I planned for her funeral that I hated the most. She died, final moment. Watching as my children screamed and prayed for God to help them, final moment. Watching as my family poured in, final moment. Waiting on the coroner to bring Bailey down, final moment. Watching as my children begged to see her just one last time, final moment. It was so many different aspects of these final moments that I wondered if God was still with me in what seemed to be *my* final moments.

Pause.

We never get to relive the moments that pass in our life. It is more difficult when it involves your precious little baby. You don't cherish these moments at all because every second that passes brings forth eternity for your baby, but a continued life on earth for you. Talk about separation anxiety! This goes beyond that. This is final moments heartache.

As the coroner went off with Bailey, family and friends gathered at our home.

Sometimes we never truly understand the impact that we have on other people until a tragedy hits. I vividly remember the amount of times my phone rang, the notifications and the many messages I received via social media. It was humbling. It was as if they felt the pain and agony my family and I were experiencing. I remember folks just staring at me as I just tried to hold it together as we sat in our home. We had run out of seats and at one point. I sat on the carpet with my legs folded beneath me. I would crack a joke here and there just to lighten the mood but my heart had left in the same body bag they carried my Bailey out in. I despised that bag. "Why did they have to put her in there as if she wasn't an innocent little baby?" I asked the coroner where they were taking her. He replied, "to have an autopsy". I asked, "How long would it take?" He assured me that we should hear something by 6pm. I kept praying that she would make a peep or some noise while in route to the pathologist and they would call me with good news. I was longing to hear "She's breathing!" As the time went on, the chance of that became less and less likely.

I tried everything possible to stay occupied while we awaited the results of her autopsy. I literally replayed everything that we did the previous day in my mind, searching for some sort of clue that proved that she wasn't feeling well. Everyone kept asking me if she was feeling sick or if I had noticed anything different about her within the last few days. I wracked my brain trying to think of something. Anything. Bailey was such a happy and healthy baby, she never even had a cold. She did have a few issues with her milk in the early weeks of her life that caused constipation. She would scream so loudly when it was time for her to have a bowel movement. I would literally tear up with her because I could tell just how bad her pain was from her unbearable cry. We changed her milk and within weeks, although the problem didn't completely go away, it did get a lot better. I then thought about her sleeping schedule and nothing was adding up. I just didn't understand how could a perfectly healthy infant fall asleep and just drift into eternity.

"I was up. I was up." I kept saying in my heart. I was so focused on my circumstances, the thought of her leaving us never crossed my mind.

"Did she cry? No, she didn't cry, I would have heard her. How could I sit up all night worrying about other issues when my baby laid lifeless in her crib? How could I ever get over this?"

DETECTIVE TIME

A few hours flew by. There was a knock at the door and this time it was the detective. He wanted me to provide him with a detailed statement as well as a re-enactment of what happened that morning. But all I really wanted to do was sit down, collect my thoughts then find a hole to go in.

Nonetheless, the detective sat at the table with me and we went through his extensive list of questions. He was a pretty nice guy, thank God. I could tell that this was not the most rewarding part of his job. My mind travelled between two places: one part of my mind was focused on the detective's questions and then the other part focused on that cold operating table that my Bailey laid on as they prepped her for the autopsy. I still had a little hope left. I prayed that at any moment we would get a call saying that she came back. Time and time again I thought about what section of Bailey's body the pathologist was working on. I finally asked the detective, "During an autopsy, do they really have to cut you?" Although I didn't know much about the process, I do know that in my anatomy and physiology classes, we studied death and how to determine timing of death basing off the Rigor Mortis scale.

He answered and demonstrated where they would cut. He said that they make an incision near the ear and would then cut to the other side of the head. I burst into tears. What was I thinking? Why did I agree to that? Surely if he had indeed opened her brain, there was no hope of her coming back. I felt so bad. How would I ever be able to face her before burial knowing these horrific details. With every question that he asked, I answered to the best of my ability but my heart was with her.

Bailey had so much hair. I imagined him having to maneuver through her beautiful curls just to see her scalp. I pictured the blood and even prayed that she didn't lose a lot. Although that may seem weird, in my mind, I figured that if she still had some fluid in her, there was still a chance.

Approximately thirty minutes later, we were done with all the questions and my tear ducts seemed to be all out of tears. But then the worse part came, the re-enactment. I dreaded this part because they brought a doll that was supposed to look and feel just like a real baby. They kept asking if I was sure that I would be ok and I kept thinking "No, I'm not ok. I am not even here right now, I'm in a pit of disbelief and at any moment, I'm praying that I wake up but since you guys insist, I want to get it over with." I sucked in my despair and headed up the stairs, two gentlemen followed me: the detective and the guy filming. Then there was a woman who I kept looking at. "How could she work such a job?" I thought. If I were her, I would be heartbroken. Yet she seemed so engulfed in her job to notice that I needed eye contact, I needed the empathy, and I didn't want to relive the moment when I found my child's lifeless body.

As the detective reached down to grab the doll out of his black bag (*A bag similar to what they carried Bailey out in*) I began to tremble. The doll looked so real, it was frightening. The detective leaned into the crib and asked me to show him everything from the time I laid her down in the crib. I felt pressured, although I knew I didn't do anything wrong. "What if I miss something? What if the cover wasn't folded right." I knew there was no way Bailey could have suffocated because she was really good at lifting and turning her head. These thoughts danced around in my mind, causing me even more pain. Occasionally he would stop me and ask the same question twice. The events of that day were playing in my head like a short-film on repeat. I kept looking at the clock to see how close we were to receiving the call from the pathologist. I just wanted answers and time was moving at turtle speed.

WHY?

Time crawled forward and there were still folks showing up. Some came just to comfort us, while others brought groceries for our home. I had my okay moments, then I hit the reality button and the despair would hit me all over again. "Lord, why didn't you allow me to miscarry? If you were going to take her away, why not in the beginning when I had minor complications?" My thoughts tormented me. In my finite mind, I thought I knew what was best for me. I knew nothing. I never got a chance to hear her laugh out loud, see her first teeth come in, her first taste of a french fry, see her try to crawl nor hear her try to utter her first words. The very thought of having to live without her made me sick to my stomach. I was deeply confused, I hated death and I didn't know what I did to cause such a thing to come upon me.

I hated that my children had to witness this. I remember them screaming and asking God to please let her live. I didn't know how to explain the death of a loved one to them. They have always been taught to pray and believe. We knew that God answers prayers, but what happens when the Lord answers in another way? How can a child understand that? My sister told me that my oldest daughter asked her if God was real? She was crying and feeling hopeless because she was praying but again, it felt like God wasn't listening. This crushed my heart and again I had to pull myself together, if not for myself, for my children. My kids needed to know that God is still God even in the midst of tragedy.

Six o'clock finally came around and I placed my phone on my chest, waiting for the call from the doctor. Deep down, I was still hoping for some life-changing news but inwardly I knew that she was already in heaven. Minutes passed by and my phone didn't ring. I dashed upstairs and began to panic. I prayed nothing was wrong, although the worse possible scenario had already occurred. I was just overly anxious and disturbed.

One thing the detective said while we were completing the paper-work that added more punches to my already tormented mind was that Bailey had passed away shortly after I laid her down. I remember questioning and asking him how was he so sure. He described different things that they look for in timing of a deceased person. I hung my head low.

The fact that she died so soon after laying her down, pierced my soul. Bailey was such a good sleeper, she was such a good baby. I just wished she could have squirmed a little or made noise that would alert us that something was wrong.

SUDDEN UNEXPLAINED INFANT DEATH

Finally, the call we had been waiting for came through. Should I answer or should I not? I felt as though, I was in a large bubble, disconnected from life yet living. Greg hurried and beckoned everyone in the house to quiet down as we went into the room to answer. "Hello", I said, my voice trembling. I was afraid. The detective's first words were, "You guys took such good care of Bailey, she was well kept together, clean and such a beautiful healthy baby. I am so sorry this has happened to you." "Thank you, ma'am", I replied. I was grateful for that compliment. They had seen past her lifeless body and noticed the love and care we gave our sweet baby girl. This meant the world to me in that moment; to look at a body and still sense love. Bailey and I had a bond that was different. She came unexpectedly and although I wasn't too excited in the beginning, I was grateful that God chose me to give birth to her. I was going through a tough season and Bailey helped me stay focused. I remember being in a really low place and at just twelve weeks, I felt her little kick. Every kick reminded me of God's goodness and pushed me to continue trusting God.

The detective confirmed that there were no bruises, no trauma, no liquid or saliva in her lungs. It was nothing. The few swabs they took were on its way to the lab and the results would take up to six weeks. Other than that, they could not find anything signifying an underlining disease or breathing difficulty that would have caused her to stop breathing. Bailey's death was deemed SIDS (Sudden Infant Death Syndrome) or SUIDS (Sudden Unexplained Infant Death). I breathed a sigh of relief and some pressure was released at that moment because I knew there was nothing that I missed as a parent. Although grief stricken, I thought and reserved in my heart at that moment "God has a plan".

Losing a child to SIDS is painful. A tug of war takes place in your mind and on one end of the rope you're grateful that your child slipped away peacefully. You come to the gripping realization that it was just his or her time to go. Then on the other end, your thoughts start to taunt you. "Perhaps if something was really wrong I'd have some closure, I'd be able to give a thorough explanation for my child's death".

We, as humans, love to have clear cut answers and explanations for everything that takes place in our lives, but sometimes life doesn't provide us with all the answers. As believers, we are to trust God and the unknown. I admonish you to believe that God truly has a plan for our lives and He alone can provide us with peace and closure.

After the call, Greg and I hugged each other and cried. We walked downstairs where the room was quiet. No one said anything. Instead, they waited for us to share the news. Greg went first and said, "It was SIDS". I slowly began to tell them about the conversation and mid-way into the details, I dropped to my knees and screamed, "No, why me?" I heard Greg crying in the corner. This was real, this was our life. Our daughter was in heaven and we were stuck on earth left to pick up the pieces to the puzzle.

That night, we didn't get any sleep. I kept jumping up and running to Bailey's crib, thinking that I heard her crying. I kept praying that God would give her back. "Please Lord, just give her back" I cried. I needed her. She needed me. How will I continue to live life without her? Lord help me!

Chapter 4

PLANNING BAILEY'S MEMORIAL

Days after Bailey's death, our house was jam packed with family, friends and loved ones. Greg and I never complained because honestly, we needed it. I often said, "You guys can spend a night if you like". I said it as a joke but I was serious. They brought us food even though we didn't have much of an appetite. Hours flew by and I sometimes forgot that I had not had a meal. When I did eat, I ate very small portions. How could I enjoy a meal when my daughter's body was stuffed somewhere in a cold room being preserved until the funeral home collected her. My appetite was with her; my thoughts were with her.

We did our research and looked at different funeral homes. After settling on the funeral home of our choice, the anxiety kicked in as I learned that the undertaker was on his way to collect Bailey's body from the morgue. I was calling every hour like clockwork to see if they had picked her up. I wanted to know every single detail. I sent one of my close friends to the funeral home to view Bailey's body. I wanted to make sure she wasn't in a state that would add to my devastation. I wanted her to look like herself. I just wanted my sweet Bailey to look as though she was sleeping. I thought on this the entire weekend until it was time for us to finally see her.

The funeral date was agreed upon. It was going to be held on a Friday July 3rd, since Saturday was the Fourth of July. On the way to the funeral home, my stomach shifted uneasily. I was filled with fear, pain, confusion and hopelessness. I was filled with emotions, yet I had no faith. I hated this. I hated death.

I was always so good in trusting the Lord when tough times came upon me. My go-to scriptures in the time of trouble were

> *A man born of a woman is of a few days and filled with trouble Job 14:1 ESV*

and

> *All things work together for the good of those that love the Lord and is called according to His purpose. Romans 8:28 ESV*

When trouble came, I knew that the Lord would work things out for me, just as His word said. God delivered me time and time again, but this time, I didn't have faith in His word. I could not see how this catastrophe could ever work out for my good. There's no good in losing a child. Every thought of good was crowded out by the smoke and the darkness that I was now walking through. No words that were faith-filled that someone spoke into my life stuck. The words flowed in one ear, sat in my mind for a time. Once I thought about Bailey those words flowed back out of the other. How could I retain a word of encouragement when I would never, ever, ever see my baby again on this side of the earth?

I looked at my other children as they sat next to me and didn't utter a word, but I could feel that they were in despair. I searched for strength, yet it appeared as if my strength ascended into heaven with Bailey. I searched for joy, yet it appeared as if my joy was taken away from me and was now resting in heaven with Bailey. I searched for peace, yet it seemed as if my peace descended to hell and the enemy held it captive, right along with my thoughts. I prayed to regain my peace, but it seemed as if the only thing I received was more pain and torment. I needed rest. Rest for my thoughts, emotions and my weary soul.

The funeral director led us to the back of the office. The back office was cold and uninviting. I tried my best to keep my composure but it was hard. There was no sympathy from the workers. Everyone was talking business and pricing. All I kept thinking was, "Lord, please help me". We finally sat down and this small, petite lady came in and sat down in her executive chair. She pulled out these large books and stacks of papers with the pricing for different funeral options. Before she could open her mouth, I asked "Where is she?" She said, "she is down stairs in the basement". "The basement, why would she be down there?" I thought. It was becoming more and more real. She asked, "Would you like for me to have them bring her up?" I answered with a soft, unsure, but sure "Yes". She made a quick call and it was back to business. The lady flipped through the book and showed us different caskets and designs. She talked about the services and what they would offer. I searched her face and wondered "Where is the empathy?" I know this is something she encounters daily, but I felt as though Bailey's death was different. I listened as they joked outside and I became even more agitated. I hated that the employees were outside laughing and telling jokes about God knows what, while I was mourning over the death of my daughter. I was hurt and I wanted everyone to feel what I felt.

I carefully described how I wanted Bailey's casket to look. I wanted a soft pink casket and a ladybug on it. We continued our search and we found the perfect casket, just like the one I pictured. It was so wrong because no one is ever excited about sorting through caskets, but I noticed that even in the midst of this trouble. God was still there and He made sure that I got the casket I wanted for my baby.

The Lord was ever so present with me even when I felt absent from my own body.

We were finally done with the details and now it was time to see Bailey. Sweat droplets formed on my forehead and my heart was racing. "Why did I ask to see her?" The feeling of anxiousness overtook me and I felt like I was about to have a panic attack. They shut the doors as they prepared to lay her on the table. With every bump or little noise that I heard, I asked if everything was okay. Everyone kept saying "calm down". I tried. I tried my hardest. Soon, a six foot tall, heavy set guy walked out and said, "she's ready". This was like a movie. This was the part where you had to hold your head down because the suspense is so great and you don't know what to expect. I stood up slowly, grabbing my friend and Greg's hand. "Lord, please don't let me break down" I prayed silently. My friend walked in first and immediately I felt a sense of peace in my spirit. It was so weird because it came so unexpectedly. As I turned the corner, I saw my sweet Bailey Nicole laying there on the table, with a white blanket up to her neck, looking like a little angel. She looked as though she was resting peacefully in her crib at home. I looked and smiled because at that moment, I knew she was with God. Not only that, I knew that heaven had to be so amazing that even though she was absent from her body, the Lord still allowed His glory to shine through her. She was so bright, and had a unique glow. It was God's glory. I stared at her and I could no longer be mad but grateful that she was ok. Although my life was flipped upside down, so was my heart. In that moment in time, I felt God's peace. Bailey had a purpose. I didn't fully understand what that purpose was at the time, but God was up to something. After about fifteen minutes in there with her, we left.

> *As I type this portion with tears in my eyes, I absolutely hate the fact that I did not get a picture of her that day. Some days I still cry, only because that was the last time I would see my daughter in a state that I recognized her in. I always say, 'let go of what you can't change', but this one is pretty tough for me.*

We left the funeral home and went to the mall to do a little shopping. I felt so much better those few hours. We got back home and it was time to find a church and put the program together. Renting the church was shockingly expensive. I was under the impression that a church would cost maybe two hundred dollars. Boy was I wrong! These prices were starting from around four hundred to five hundred dollars. Nonetheless, the Lord worked everything out perfectly. My family and friends chipped in to help cover some of the funeral expenses. I found Bailey the perfect dress on Amazon and I was very happy about that. Her dress was soft pink at the top and the bottom was white with black trim. It was everything I wanted it to be. I really wanted her dress to match her casket. I also found her a little gold angel necklace for an accessory.

Although her funeral was scheduled for Friday, the funeral home requested that she be dressed by Wednesday. That Wednesday morning, we left to meet our pastor and to pay for the church. We arrived at the desk and started talking to the lady who was collecting the check. Midway into the conversation she got teary eyed. She had just lost her son a few months back. She said that our story brought back the emotions she felt during her process. That day, God connected us. We were two women who loved Jesus and were depending on His strength to get by. I was happy that I got the opportunity to meet that lady and her story helped ease my pain just a bit.

God did a pretty good job in sending me reminders of His presence. No matter how many times I tried to ignore His reminders or bury them under my grief, He always made it clear that He was still in control.

I had a list of questions that I needed to ask the mortician, mainly about her embalming. I had stressed the fact that I really wanted Bailey to look like herself. She was a bright baby. I've witnessed a few deceased people turn a dark grey or blackish color after the embalming process. The mortician advised me that Bailey's color changed a little but not too much. It was in that moment that I deeply regretted not getting a photo of Bailey before the process started.

The following day, everything flowed smoothly and I was anxious to see how Bailey's little outfit came together. I kept replaying how things would go in my head. I gave myself little pep talks and said, "I will be strong". We finally received the call to go do our last viewing and again, I had that uneasy feeling. We walked in the building and were greeted by the staff. I peeked in the room and immediately started wailing. "Who is she? That's not Bailey. I asked you guys not to ruin my daughter. OMG, what did you do to her ear? Why is it crooked?" I cried hysterically. The mortician said that the lighting was bad and they would exchange it. It was not the lighting, it was the embalming fluid. Whatever process they used to preserve the body did not work for my baby and it hurt. I heard everyone scrambling and I also sensed their empathy. They could tell that I was completely crushed in my soul.

Bailey's skin complexion turned dark grey. They applied so much makeup to her skin, she didn't even look like a baby. Her forehead was protruding outwards, her fingers were flat and her ear looked crooked. "This will be a closed casket. I will not allow my daughter to be seen like this", I cried. The employees hooked up some more lights which highlighted the careless mistakes even more. Everyone was asking me to calm down but I couldn't, this was a catastrophe. The mortician pulled me aside and very quietly she asked what would I like her to do. I was not overreacting, or being dramatic, I was deeply hurt. "Please remove the makeup, all of it", I said. She went downstairs to get the makeup bag. Greg called his grandmother for her assistance since she was a makeup artist. The mortician began to wipe Bailey's face, but something still didn't look right. "What did you guys embalm her with?" She tried to explain the process to me but it was hard for me to receive what she was saying because I asked them to please be careful with her. Suddenly, I began to feel this blanket of peace and comfort and it was like the Lord reassured me that this was just a body. The Holy Spirit reminded me that Bailey was in heaven and on that table, was only her shell. Bailey was still as beautiful as ever in heaven. I asked the Lord to give me direction, and He did. I kicked into mommy mode and I asked for a comb, her make-up bag, mascara and some lip gloss. I pulled a headband out of my bag and used that to cover up the side of her face that looked disproportioned. I brushed her hair and wiped off some more of the make-up. Although I was upset, I also knew there was nothing I could do besides work forward or have a closed casket. I knew my children needed to see her one last time so that was not an option. I added mascara to her eyelashes and I was in awe of how long they were. "Baby lotion, I need baby lotion", I asked. She had this smell that wasn't bad but I didn't like it. I wanted her to smell like my baby again. I did my best to groom her and make her presentable. Time and time again, I ran my hand against her cold body and I cringed in the inside. I was cringing, not in disgust but in a way that churned my grief like butter. Most people have butterflies when they are in love or meet the person of their dreams. During this moment, I had bats in the pit of my stomach because I was preparing to bury my daughter. The fear of it all was felt in every sharp flutter in my gut. After the final viewing, we went home to prepare for the funeral the following morning.

Chapter 5

WELL ACQUAINTED WITH PAIN

All this time, I thought I knew pain. I have experienced the loss of several family members including my dad as mentioned in Chapter one. My family shared with me that when I was a young girl, my father would come around and bring me money. On one occasion, he bought me a bike. I have no recollection of it. I prayed for many years to just see a picture of him. I even paid the V.A. for his medical records hoping to at least visualize what he was like. I still came up with nothing. I never understood why the Lord allowed me not to find any pictures of him. That is why my soul was crushed when I found out he was dead. I thought I would never recover, but I did.

Life can sometimes be filled with hardship, disappointments and uncertainties. I was beginning to understand this. Pain wasn't new to me. I've suffered and endured over and over again. Every time I reflected on the pain and hurt that was caused during those painful seasons of my life, my heart would feel as though it was being shattered all over again. Abuse.

Yes, abuse. I know the pain of being verbally and physically attacked as well and not knowing if or how I would be able to cover up the marks not only on my body, but mentally and emotionally. But Bailey's death pierced me to the core. If I took all those instances and stirred them in a pot, it still could not compare to this agonizing pain of losing my daughter.

I thought on the days when I was at my lowest point, with no one to fully share the extent of the things I was going through with. I thought on how I would drive to the park, park my car away from traffic and just cry. The tormenting pain of preparing the burial of a life that barely started, the torture of watching her as she lay in her casket, lifeless was indeed, crippling.

Everything was happening so quickly; all the preparations and funeral arrangements gave me little time to sit and mourn.

> *One thing I noticed looking back, you don't feel the full extent of the pain during that first week or so because you are surrounded with family and friends. You are so busy chatting and sharing past stories that you feel as though you will be alright. Then there are the other moments when everyone is silent and you realize that your baby is gone and you just weep.*

I purchased two outfits to wear to choose from and I was still indecisive. I didn't know what to wear. Bailey's dress was soft-pink, black and white, so we decided to color coordinate. A few weeks ago, I purchased a black skirt to wear to my graduation. At the last minute I decided not to wear it. I grabbed a plastic bag, tied it up and sat it underneath my fish tank in hopes to return it. The morning of the funeral, after trying on several outfits, nothing seemed to work. I had dropped some weight in those few days and it was very obvious. I was getting so frustrated and then a thought came to my mind, "what about that black skirt, try that on, it'll work". I hurried to the bag and tried it on and it fit perfectly. I thanked the Lord for reminding me of that and for allowing me to hold on to it when I wanted to return it. Honestly, I was very grateful and I knew that the Lord was working.

> *It is so amazing how God works. He has you purchasing items and doing small things way ahead of time. Unbeknownst to you, He is always prepping you for what's to come.*

God is always looking out for us and preparing us for our trials. For Him to think on a detail as small as what I was going to wear was enough to comfort my heart. As the morning progressed, it got more hectic. Greg left to go to the church to make sure that everything flowed smoothly. My family met me at the house and we sat together to wait on the limousine. I was so happy to see my sisters, brothers, nieces and nephews. Although they were with me all week, today was different. I needed them. The kids were so excited to ride in the limo that they couldn't wait for it to pull up. The adults were super nervous and none of us really knew what to expect. We knew it would hurt, we just didn't know how bad or how we would react to the pain.

With every smile and with every joke there was also this moment of silence. We couldn't believe that we were really headed to Bailey's funeral. The limo pulled up and the kids ran out the door, over the moon excited, while my heart was almost about to jump out of my chest. I kept calling Greg to check in to see how things were going. My other close friend was also there, assisting with setting things up. My stomach shifted uneasily as we approached the church. With each turn, I felt so alone. I kept praying for peace and to still my heart to make it through the service. I needed God now, more than I ever needed Him before. Those words probably never left my lips but I know that my heart cried out for Him.

As we pulled into the church, I couldn't believe my eyes. The young lady that Greg had been having an affair with was leaving the parking lot. Did she really view my daughter's body? How low of her! Here I am preparing to say goodbye to my daughter for forever and I can't even do that without drama. Anger and disbelief swelled in my heart and I couldn't jump out the limo fast enough. I went into the church, frantically searching for Greg. I burst through the men's bathroom to confront him about what I saw. Words escaped me and rage filled my mind. I wanted to scream. I began to speak to him as lowly as someone in my shoes could possibly have. It was hard for me to formulate the right words. I just couldn't understand how someone could be so disrespectful! Why would she come to my daughter's funeral? He pretended as if he didn't know what was going on but deep in my heart, I knew that he was aware. I pulled myself together and we both walked out the bathroom. This was another instance where I had to pretend like everything was ok, just to save face. His face. The people who recognized her were angry as well, but out of respect for me, everyone remained calmed.

> *Reflecting back, long after forgiving the mistress and putting the past behind, it still makes no sense to me. How could someone who has hurt your family in more ways than one, show up at my daughter's funeral and not think about the hurt that it would cause me!*

I realized that the enemy is always working and when it comes to those battles, I try not to lift a finger. The Lord is way better at handling people than I could ever be. I prayed in my heart as I walked down the hall to search for my mom. Walking in the lobby, I saw her and I immediately fell on her shoulders weeping. My daughter and nieces had gone into the sanctuary and viewed her body. They were crying as well. Briyah, my youngest, kept asking "Why is she so dirty? Why didn't they clean her off?" The color of her skin after the embalming had changed so much that my daughter thought that she had been in the dirt. Talk about a crushing statement.

More people flooded the sanctuary and I knew I needed to pull myself together. I would smile and wave when someone called my name or waved for my attention, but at that moment I wasn't in the mood for being social. I love to chat and talk to people, especially when I haven't seen them in a while, but that day was hard. I had no words for anyone.

We lined up so that we could enter the funeral procession. Our Pastor was in the front, while our family lined up behind us. We walked in slowly as he read Psalm 23.

> *The Lord is my shepherd; I shall not want.*
> *He makes me lie down in green pastures.*
> *He leads me beside still waters.*
> *He restores my soul.*
> *He leads me in paths of righteousness*
> *for his name's sake.*
> *Even though I walk through the valley of the*
> *shadow of death,*
> *I will fear no evil,*
> *for you are with me;*
> *your rod and your staff,*
> *they comfort me.*
> *You prepare a table before me*
> *in the presence of my enemies;*

you anoint my head with oil;
my cup overflows.
Surely goodness and mercy shall follow me
all the days of my life,
and I shall dwell in the house of the Lord
forever. (ESV)

I kept my eyes straight in front of me. The left side of the church was filled with friends, friends of friends and co-workers. Sympathy and sadness thickened the atmosphere. No one made a sound. The organist played as the Pastor continued with the reading of the scripture. Once we sat down, I felt myself sink down into my chair. I didn't look back at all. Before the ceremony even started, the tears begin to flow. I thought, "Okay Lord, we are here. Please work your miracle and bring her back to life or at least wake me up from this nightmare". The program picked up and so did my reality check. The tears flowed even more.

We had a few singers, praise dancers, a long list of condolence letters and even a few people who stood up to encourage our hearts yet still, I couldn't shake the hopelessness. Once the Pastor stood up to preach, I felt a small sense of peace but as soon as they opened the casket, like a vapor, that peace went out the window and my family and I wept. The crowd lined up to view the body and I could hardly look anyone in the face. My heart was in heaven, searching for the Lord and begging for comfort. Everyone who walked around to view her body, stopped to hug me. Shortly after, my cousins came and stood between the aisle and to give me some relief. I needed those hugs but they became overwhelming for me.

> *All my life I spoke about God being a Healer and how we must trust Him in every circumstance, yet I felt as though, I was failing God and most importantly, that my faith had failed me.*

It was our turn to go to the casket and I felt my knees buckling as I stared at her for the final time. The bats began to overtake the pit of my stomach again and I let out this agonizing cry that I know touched the hearts of God's angels.

The funeral home started to rush us because we were nearing the time of her burial but all I wanted to do was wait. Wait on God to do the miraculous. Wait on God to do, what I knew He wouldn't and that's give her back. As we ended, Greg picked up her little casket and walked her out to the funeral car. I followed close behind him and jumped right into the limousine. I didn't have a single piece of energy to give to anyone at that point. I was done.

The ride to the cemetery was long, I remember looking back at the cars that were trailing us. It brought my heart a tiny bit of gladness knowing just how much support we had for Bailey. In just four short months, she touched the hearts of thousands. I know that everyone who surrounded us during that season wished that they could have done more but the simple posts, cards, text, phone calls etc. meant more than they would probably ever know. Thank you, guys, again!

When the limo pulled up and we stepped out, my tears were all dried and I began to feel a little bit better. As they settled Bailey's casket in, before the final remarks, I glanced at her casket. Can you believe that there was a lady bug, one of the most beautiful colored lady bugs I had ever seen, crawling on her casket! I could hardly contain myself. I noticed everyone looking at me staring and all I could do was look up to heaven and thank my Father, Jesus Christ, for comforting me and letting me know that everything was going to be alright. Not only had God got me through one of the toughest funerals in my life, He had also shown me so many wonderful signs reassuring me that this was not only the end of one chapter, but a beginning of another.

I knew that if I continued to walk with Him on this journey, though it was hard, that He would keep His promise to me and work this loss out for my good.

I reflected on the days prior when the cemetery drove us out to her plot. While there, Greg and I saw a lady bug walking on her burial plot. "Was this by chance?" Maybe, but today proved that it was divine. God loves us. He loves us so much that even when we are in the lowest points of our life, He will leave His footprints all around so that we can grasp His presence. Could God have brought Bailey back? Absolutely. At this very moment, if He called out to her and said 'rise', her soul and spirit would reunite and she would rise just as He commanded. Bailey continuing to live on earth was just not in His will. Although it hurt me to the core, ultimately, I had no control over His plan for her life.

> *If you have experienced such a loss, just know, God knows far more than we would ever know. The Bible says, "For my thoughts are not your thoughts, neither are your ways my ways, saith the Lord (Isaiah 55:8 KJV)." We couldn't understand Him fully if we tried. What we can understand and grab a hold to is this. He promised to never leave us or forsake us so even while you are facing this trial, He is right there.*

Trust me, I know the feeling of feeling forsaken. Once we returned to the repass, I cried and cried and cried some more. I kept shouting how no one understood what I was going through. I kept trying to explain how alone I felt. Everyone else was joking and chowing down on chicken while I was just wanting to go and dig a hole for myself. I felt forsaken. The enemy's job is to make us "feel" this way because he knows there is no hope for one who feels hopeless or forsaken. That is why it is so important not to base our reality off of what we feel. Feelings make a great servant but a horrible master. My feelings that day had me accusing God of something that is not even in His word and that is contrary to His very character and attributes. I finally settled down and began to mingle with my family. I spoke with my cousin and listened as she encouraged my heart while in her grief. She had just buried her husband a few weeks before Bailey passed away. I empathized with her because I knew it had to be tough for her to come to Bailey's funeral and I could only imagine the memories that played in her mind as the service went on.

Death is hard, especially when it is unexpected.

Chapter 6

SINK OR SWIM

After the funeral, everyone's lives went back to normal, but I was still stuck. Bailey's funeral was on the 3rd of the July so that following day, my family and I spent the day at my brother's home. I had my moments when I got teary eyed but being in the company of my family kept me busy, so it wasn't too bad. Monday rolled around, and my phone magically stopped ringing as often. Hardly anyone came over to visit and everyone literally carried on with their lives. The more I sat around the house, the heavier I felt. I didn't get up to move any of Bailey's things. Her swing was still nestled in the corner along with her baby bag and other items she used. Her clothes, milk, juice, bassinet and everything else were right where she left it. I had no plans of rearranging anything. I couldn't bear to do it. Looking at her belongings day in and day out made me sad, but it also brought me some comfort. I refused to sleep in my bedroom since the night of Bailey's incident. The thought of her bare bed made me cringe. The police department stripped her bedding and took everything that was in her crib the morning she passed away. It was literally bare, no baby, no comforter. Bare.

Once things started to settle down, everything became like a cloud of smoke. My children stayed at my mom's house for a while and then at my sister's. I'm so thankful that they offered to keep an eye on them since I was not in a good place. Of course, I would never harm them. I just really needed time to think and reflect. My mind was playing its own game of tug of war and I was stuck again asking the Lord, "Why me?" The battles in my mind got so intense until I almost had a nervous break-down on two separate occasions. I remember sitting on the couch, trying my hardest to remember Bailey's face, but for some reason I couldn't. (*This was a stage in my grief where I couldn't picture her face in my mind. I had to look at a picture to know what she looked like*). I was devastated. I also tried to remember the names of my other children, but failed. Immediately, I started panicking and soon I was hyperventilating. I tried my best to repeat "The blood of Jesus" and soon enough I was able to control my breathing. I knew then that the enemy was trying to take my mind because he knew if he had my mind he would have me. Although I was frightened, the more I prayed for the blood of Jesus to cover my mind, the more I began to settle down and collect my thoughts. There was another time when I was on the road with Greg traveling to Myrtle Beach.

While driving down the highway I tried to picture Bailey in my mind and then all of a sudden, my thoughts went completely blank and I went into panic mode. I didn't know what to do. I refused to tell Greg because he probably would've thought I was crazy or try to send me to the nut house. Instead, I did what I knew to do; I prayed. I began to ask the Lord to help me and cover my mind with His blood once again. I decided that night that I wouldn't think so hard on something like that ever again. Maybe the Lord was preventing me from seeing her to protect me, or maybe my grief was so overwhelming that her beautiful little face couldn't surface in my gloom-ridden thoughts. There was a warzone going on in my mind and little Bailey didn't deserve to be caught in the middle of it.

> *Looking back, I now understand that **grief** had masked her face in my mind. It's the same tactic that I learned as a little girl. I buried my pain deep in my heart so that I wouldn't have to face it. I believe my mind buried her little face.*

The days flew by rather quickly. Greg was leaving and getting back to the things he loved to do while I sat at home depressed. Little problems appeared here and there in our marriage and it was tough for me to fight that battle and grieve at the same time. Instead, I chose to go into the basement or sit in my bathroom on the floor and just weep.

That's all my strength allowed me to do. I perfected the art of "pulling myself together" when someone called. I would listen as the caller encouraged me on the other line. I was hopeful for a minute or two and after the call my hope disappeared again.

One night, I visited Greg at the rink. We had just had an argument and I was so upset with him that I went where he was. Little did I know that I would leave that night having got into a whole altercation that would forever change the way I react to someone who so desperately needed prayer and grace, just as I did. I had a conversation with someone there. Although I know he didn't mean any harm, he told me that I did not look like myself, in fact, he said, I looked bad. He said that I used to be beautiful and that he can tell life was taking a toll on me. He wasn't referring to my grief. He was talking about me trying to keep tabs on Greg. He looked me in my eyes and said, "Take care of yourself". Those words dug deep into my heart. I said my goodbyes and headed out to my car. The same young lady that Greg was having an affair with came out shortly after. We exchanged words and before I knew it, we were fighting. Greg came out and so did others. I got in my car to leave and I called my family to meet me at my house. That was it, I was leaving. I could not believe Greg went back to skating and did not follow or make sure I was ok.

I came home a few days later because Greg was begging me to come home and start over. Deep down I knew that it was a mistake but I still wanted to give it another try. I was caught up in this web of dysfunction.

That same week, my family and I decided to go on a week and a half long spontaneous road trip. Our first stop was Niagara Falls. It was incredibly beautiful and peaceful there. I watched closely as the water fell off the cliff and into the deep ocean, then I thought of my life. I watched the falls and used it as an analogy for my life. I imagined the water being all of my hard times and the tears that flowed through my heart. The point where the falls drop off is where my life was at now. It had dropped off to this low place.

All of the people standing around and watching were the folks that were amazed by my strength. But no one understood what was in that water and the flow of it. All they saw was the beauty of me remaining hopeful outwardly.

We stayed there for hours and I thought it would be a wonderful idea for us to cross over to Canada, so we did just that. I had no idea that we needed either our birth certificates or passport to cross over. It wasn't until we got to the gate we realized that we had done something illegal. After a series of questions we were told to go into the customs building and begin the long process of trying to get back into the U.S. They were particularly hard on Greg because he was a felon. We couldn't eat or anything. At one point, they allowed me to go to the car to get my purse and I saw that they had searched the car.

I couldn't believe this was happening, I wasn't too worried but fear began to creep in. What if they don't allow us to move. If I couldn't remember anything else, I knew that in those moments I needed to pray. That's what I did, I prayed fervently. Finally, after hours of being watched in a little room, we were released. We had very strict orders and they were not the nicest people. I believe that they thought we were lying about not knowing that we needed travel documentation. I cared nothing about their attitude, I was just grateful that the Lord had heard and answered my prayer. After leaving Canada, we headed to downtown New York. The trip got even more interesting as we ran into toll booth after toll booth. Greg and I laughed as we were paying them, hysterically, we were like two little teenagers back in the day. We couldn't understand how the residents survived living in a state like that.

New York was beyond fascinating. I believe that the city lights and tall monumental buildings were enough to lighten anyone's mood. While on the trip, our grief would come in waves. We would drive a few hours laughing and joking. Then, in the midst of our conversation, something as small as a phrase or a word would remind us of Bailey. We were dim in spirit but upon arriving in Times Square, we felt the life that was there. Everyone was moving and moving fast, at that. Traffic was bumper to bumper. Every five feet there were unique individuals on the sidewalks doing something to help brighten the day. As the night approached, we thought things would slow down, but it never did. We visited several stores including Toys R Us. The kids really enjoyed it there because they had a Ferris wheel in the inside. It was an amazing day! We even found a little street name sign with Bailey's name on it. There were so many little shops and things to do that it totally whisked us away from our reality. That night we hopped back in the car and set out for a hotel. We had no idea that the rooms were so expensive and not only that but some hotels had options to share rooms with other people. We thought it would be best if we drove to a rest stop and catch up on some sleep before heading back to Virginia. The following day, we were on the road again. We traveled through several states and visited the different monuments. The open road helped to clear my mind. I believe that the Lord orchestrated this trip. He used this trip to help me to relax, reflect and minister to the depths of my heart.

We made it in to Virginia and stayed there for a few days. After the exciting trip, we were on our way back home. The kids quickly got settled in, and Greg and I finally came up to the bedroom to sleep. For the first time in a long time, my room was incredibly peaceful.

I noticed this peace as the days went on and I thought, the Lord took Bailey but He left an abundance of His peace. Still to this day, that peace still resides in here.

You don't have many choices when you're in the valley, fighting the good fight of faith to get to the mountain top. All you have is faith and the hope that if you put one foot in front of the other, that God would carry you through. Life sometimes feels like death. Not a physical death, but one that emotionally wrecks us. The psalmist David said it this way, *"yea, though I walk through the valley of the shadow of death, I will fear no evil: for thou art with me; thy rod and thy staff they comfort me."* Psalms 23:4 KJV

God was comforting me when I felt like I was drowning in the midst of my despair. God was keeping me afloat. I was so embarrassed by the run in I had with Greg's mistress that I almost didn't share it with you. I knew better. But, I am human and the anger and pain that I felt in those moments caused me to fight my own battle with her. I lost that battle that day. Not by punches but by not trusting God to render vengeance on my behalf. I said some ugly things that day, words that I thought were no longer in my vocabulary. The Lord allowed me to see that under that rug were all the other grievances from life; toxic words lived there and would later need to be purged out as well. This was by far the darkest and longest journey I've ever had to embark on but I am so grateful that I did not sink in my mistakes. Instead, I learned a valuable lesson. To swim. I prayed for my enemies and God strengthened me. He allowed me to jump in the river of cleansing that was in that valley and swim to the other side. On the other side of that valley was my mountain and God delivered me. He delivered me from my embarrassment, my fear of judgement and from pain. Those tears that I cried silently were not in vain. Thou I walked through the valley of what I thought was death, it was really only a shadow. It was a dark shadow that could not defeat me because God had already given me victory. God has given you victory as well. If you've ever gone through an affair, got caught up in the middle of drama or have experienced an unfavorable situation while grieving, just know that you are not alone. If you are too embarrassed to share, don't be. I too, walked that long valley and swam in the waters of despair. God did not allow me to sink, I still chose His ways, walked in obedience and swam to my greater purpose!

GRIEF ON THE BACK BURNER

Have you ever felt like your heart was torn into two? You want to hurt and deal with the pain of one situation while other circumstances are pulling at your heart as well. I found myself in this situation for months after the altercation. The heart on the cover depicts what my heart felt like after Bailey's death. I was torn; one part of me wanted to grieve for my daughter even months after her death. My grief for her had to be put on the back burner. I couldn't focus on Bailey's death because the grief from my marriage far outweighed her death. Although this sounds backwards, it was my truth and my reality. I missed Bailey and Lord knows I wanted her back with every fiber in my being. But, I knew that I could not bring her back, this knowledge even brought me a little peace.

My marriage, on the other hand, was right before me. I felt it slipping away with every slammed door, every argument. Every time I heard the wheels of his car squeal away, a part of my heart followed. It was as if I was watching a part of my life die. I watched the demise. On the days when the pain was so intense from his affairs, I felt a stabbing pain in my chest. Then I thought on Bailey and all of it would completely overwhelm me. Of course, he wasn't being whisked into eternity, but the love we once shared was being buried six feet under, never to return.

It was during those dark nights that God began to work the principles of trust into my heart. I began to see what true trust meant. It was me, giving God my hurt and pain and trusting that He would replace it with healing. It was me, giving God my hopelessness and waiting in expectation that He would replace it with hope. It was me, giving Him every question that I needed answers to and trusting that He would replace those questions with His divine understanding of my life. You see, that's the principle of trust, plain and simple. It is you giving God everything; emptying yourself of yourself and sitting empty; waiting as He fills you up with His will and His plan. It's trusting that He is the light in your darkness. It is trusting that He is the fabric in our heart and He is involved in every intricate part. Not only is God in the details, but His love is that stitch that weaves our hearts back together. It is the thread that connects our hearts back together that will last until we get to heaven if we rely on Christ's love.

I know that the healing for my grief from loss came after my healing from the grief of life (my childhood and marriage). I believe many women put their grief on the back burner while busying ourselves with the cares of this life. We scroll through social media, we shop, we eat, we do whatever is necessary to keep us from dealing with our pain. If this is you, today, I want you to pause. Take a break from reading and go find a quiet place to pray. Ask God to expose every grievance that you have placed on the back burner. You must heal, my sister or brother! It is necessary! I know you don't understand why you have had to face such hardship and honestly, I don't have the answers either. God does. He may not reveal them to you but in time, everything will come together. If not on earth, in heaven.

I learned the hard way that not dealing with issues or trying to wish them away only makes matters in your heart worse. I learned as I laid in the bed, silently crying, that I cannot make excuses any longer. Neither can you. Give God your mistakes and He will give you a testimony. Give God your fears and He will give you faith. Give God your rejection and He will show you true love. Give God your spouse and marital problems and He will give you a strategy to turn his heart (if it's His will). Give God the pain from your divorce and He will give you that marriage that you always dreamed about. But first, you must deal with everything that is tucked away on the backburner.

God stands ready and willing to walk you through to your healing. This is not an overnight process. I know that we are used to popcorn results. In other words, we want to get from heartbroken to healed in a matter of moments. But that is not how God works. There is always a journey from point A to point B. If you will take the first step, I promise that God will go before you, all the while holding your hand, walking with you and He will even clean the residue from behind you.

Chapter 7

PAIN INTO PURPOSE

One day, I was down stairs washing and talking to the Lord as I always do. I looked over in the corner and noticed that Bailey's first little dress that she wore to church was hanging up. I picked it up, held it to my chest and began to weep. I literally felt the sting this time. I closed my eyes and saw this vision of me walking out on stage. I was a speaker and there were thousands of women in the audience. While crying, I thought to myself "OMG, what just happened?" My tears began to dry and I began to ponder on what just happened. I shared this vision with a few others but a part of me was still afraid that folks would think that I was crazy. I was ignorant to the fact that the Lord still speaks to His people through dreams and visions.

A few weeks had passed, and Greg was taking my kids over to their Grandma's house. I helped my daughter Briyah find her shoes and once they left out, I locked the door and dashed to the bathroom. I felt God tugging on my heart and before I could make it to the bathroom, I fell to my knees in surrender. I cried out to the Lord, and asked Him to forgive me for not trusting Him. "Lord, You allowed this and I know you'll help me get through this. You knew it would be too great of a burden for me to bear. I can't take it anymore, please just give me peace. I need Your strength", I whispered. I repented for my sins and my prayer to God came from a sincere but broken place. Immediately, I felt a weight lift off me. God was reconstructing and giving me the peace I prayed for. Soon, my mind was clear. The battle that I was fighting for months was over and all it took was truly surrendering and crying out to my Heavenly Father. I looked in the mirror and realized how small I got; my jaw was sinking in and I didn't look like the Bettye I was a few months ago. That guy was right! I had allowed the enemy to rule and reign in my life and over my situation for far too long. I had to pull myself together, cast my cares and worries on God and leave them there. It was time to fight. I pulled out my Bible and notepad and I began to read and use the tools that God gave me. I studied the life of Joseph and while I studied the Holy Spirit ministered to me. I highlighted every high point in his journey as well as the lows. More importantly, I noticed how God was strategic in teaching Joseph key life lessons that helped in the future all the while he was still serving as a prisoner. Joseph didn't understand everything that was going on but he was determined to trust God.

God showed Joseph a dream, but Joseph had to go through a painful but necessary process. His story encouraged me to hold on to my vision and prompted me to trust God through the process.

The following day, I was sitting on the couch and smiled to myself because it was Bailey's two-month mark in heaven. The Lord put it on my heart to create a video for her. I didn't know how or what I would do, I just had to do it. I compiled some of my favorite photos of her and I added a nice song. Within thirty minutes, I created a short, sweet video that I uploaded onto Facebook. I posted it and to my surprise, it went viral. Within a week, the post had over one million views. I couldn't believe it! I was receiving tons of messages and support from complete strangers. The following day, the Lord told me to start a page in honor of Bailey and name it *Bailey's Dash.* The dash, simply meaning her space on earth. This idea sparked from the design on her funeral program. My Pastor always referenced "the dash that is between your birth and death date on your tombstone". Our birthdate and the death date are important, but more important than anything is the dash, meaning the life that you lived. Bailey's life was short, but it was purposeful so we thought that was perfect. So here it is, just two months after her passing the Lord had already started working things out for the good.

One may say, "How is that good? You got a few hits and created a page". To that person I would say, "After my first transparent post on grief, hundreds of women began to message me and open up about the death of their infants. Women from all over the country were finding healing and comfort through Bailey's Dash page". At the end of each post, I would always try and encourage the hearts of the readers all the while trusting those same words to uplift my own heart. I read this scripture often and watch as it was manifested in my own life. 2 Corinthians 1:3-4 [3] *Blessed be the God and Father of our Lord Jesus Christ, the Father of mercies and God of all comfort,* [4] *who comforts us in all our affliction, so that we may be able to comfort those who are in any affliction, with the comfort with which we ourselves are comforted by God.* This was so real for me. I could feel the chills as the messages poured in. All Glory was unto God. I found my passion for writing. After all these years, I never knew of the love I had for writing and being transparent. I remember when I was a teenager, I would write all the time in this little journal that my mom bought. Once she found it and read it, the embarrassment I felt in my young heart caused me to ditch the pen and paper. Instead, I carried my writings in my heart. But once I created the Dash page, I noticed that when I write, the Holy Spirit guides my thoughts and transforms them into words. Sometimes I don't even remember what I typed. Pain has its way of impregnating you with purpose but in the midst of it, healing is birthed. During this season, I found my love for God's word and teaching it again. If you would have asked me what I wanted to be as a little girl, I would have said a preacher's wife and a Bible teacher. I loved God and I wanted to teach and lead His people (women in particular). During grief, that ignited a fire that I had let die a long time ago, not the first lady part but the teaching. I wanted to teach the word of God and have a radio show that encouraged the hearts of broken hearted women all over the world. I planned to travel the world sharing the gospel and how God took my 'woe' and turned it into 'wow', all for His glory and the testimony that Jesus heals. I truly believe what is from the heart, reaches the heart and if God allowed me to walk through these difficulties, surely it was because He wanted to use my life to show someone else that they too can overcome. As the Lord continues to develop your purpose know that everything does not have to be perfect in order for you to serve and operate in that purpose. You just have to begin. Start where you are and trust that God will get you to where He is taking you. When you use your talents and gifts to pour into others, you are also pouring into your own soil. The Bible says this in Proverbs 11:25 ESV *"Whoever brings blessing will be enriched, and one who waters will himself be watered."* The blessing that you bring is allowing the Lord to develop and use the talent He has given you for His purpose so that you can serve others. We all have a purpose and if you are struggling with knowing what your purpose is, I admonish you to pray and seek God concerning it. God will reveal it to you.

I didn't find purpose; in God's eyes my purpose was never lost. I just had to shift gears and refocus my attention on heaven and trust God completely with my life, surrendering it all.

> *I always say, "We live life forward but we understand it backwards". We never fully understand why God allows certain things to happen but in retrospect it is all part of God's giant puzzle that He continues to piece together day by day. All of it is a part of purpose. It is important that our focus remains on God. No matter what our circumstances look like, God is faithful. All things, including mistakes, lies, betrayal, loss, grief, financial difficulties, rejection work together for our good!*

Chapter 8

NEW NORMAL

When people are experiencing the different stages of grief, it's not always easy to share or express how you truly feel. You have a new normal and honestly, it's sometimes hard to even put into words the pain that follows you everywhere you go after losing a child. Everything that you do, reminds you of your baby. If you go to the grocery store, babies are there shopping with their mothers. You turn on the TV, there is a commercial advertising the newest baby products. You surf the web and there is always someone making a pregnancy announcement or having a gender reveal party. If I can be honest, it gets overwhelming at times. There will be times when you constantly have to remind yourself to trust God and remain positive. This truth can be very tough in the moments when all you want to do is see your baby. Greg and I agreed to do something as a couple to help lighten the mood, so we went to Texas Road House to eat. We sat and talked for a while as we waited for the server to bring out our food. Greg went into the restroom, and shortly after a couple entered the restaurant with their young baby. I couldn't help but look. The baby was making all sorts of cooing sounds that reminded me of Bailey and before I knew it my eyes welled up with tears. Greg came out the bathroom and he immediately asked, "What's wrong?". I pointed behind me. The baby started cooing again and his tears began to flow as well. By the time, we received our food we had to ask the waiter to box it up, our appetite was boxed in with that food. We couldn't eat after that. That was just one instance, but there were many more waves of grief that I was experiencing in my New Normal. Most times the tears still come, but you'll learn how to hold them in until you get to a private place to release them.

I cried so much during those early days. I would often joke and say that my tear ducts would dry out one day. Clearly that never happened. When the pain would semi ease, so would my tears.

DIFFERENT STAGES OF GRIEF

There are many different aspects of grief and no two people grieve the same. The stages that I went through may not look the same as someone else's that dealt with the same situation and that's ok. I believe that when we try and line up our emotions at a certain time in our grief with someone else's, it can conflict with our truth. So, I will go through the different emotions I experienced in hopes that it will help encourage you during this season.

DENIAL

For me, in the very beginning I was in **denial**. With my eyes, I saw that Bailey was gone but my mind couldn't comprehend it and my heart wouldn't let her go. If you noticed in the previous chapters, I waited expectantly for a miracle. I had hope all the way up until they buried her. Even then, I thought maybe, while the guy was plowing where she was about to be buried, he would hear a faint cry and it would be Bailey. I wanted that to be my truth so badly that it brought more emotional stress on me.

> *It is important to hang onto hope but don't cling so tightly that you live in denial. Faith is good and we should always have faith that God can restore life. When you pray, ask for God's will to be done above all else. I prayed and cried for a miracle but I brought more confusion and pain to myself because I didn't accept what God was doing. Yes, I did need a miracle but the miracle involved God healing me from the brokenness that had shattered my life the day she left.*

ANGRY

A few weeks after the burial, I became **angry**. I was angry at myself for believing that the Lord would bring her back. I would click on different sites that spoke about SIDS and that immediately aroused my anger. As I read through the articles, my heart would start racing then I would quickly click it off. How dare they mention these things that all moms had done to care for their child. Most articles would give these two guidelines to prevent SIDS...

- Don't put your baby to sleep on his stomach.
- DON'T put blankets or toys in the crib.

Although we all know preventive measures should be taken, what do you tell a Mom whose infant was lying on her back when they passed away? Or a mother who left the crib empty or better yet a mother whose infant passed while the mom cradled him or her? I thought on teenagers and adults who passed away in their sleep. There are no preventive measures that are posted for their age range and the autopsy report is usually deemed "natural causes". None of this made sense to me and I prayed and ask God for understanding.

I know as life progresses we learn more about humanity and how to prevent certain illnesses but in this case, it was different. It was different because I knew deep in my heart *(my own conviction)* most of the listed precautions could not prevent SIDS. If it could, it wouldn't have been called "Sudden & unexplained". I felt as though the articles partially put the blame on me.

> *Always follow the proper precautions when caring*
> *for your newborn. My point is that if you know*
> *that you did everything in a healthy and safe*

way, don't allow a website to make you feel as if you had done something differently the tragedy would've been prevented.

Then, in came the **what if's** once again. What if I had not laid her down? What if I would have let her sleep with me that night? Why didn't I know something was wrong (*this was a big one for me*)? What if she cried and I did not hear her? What if I would have done this or did that? I played all these scenarios in my mind wondering what if I would have done things differently, would she still be alive. I remember a few weeks after her funeral, I went to the mall. I was speaking with a jeweler that Greg and I would chat with often. He asked me how Bailey was doing and I had to break the news to him that Bailey was no longer with us. His facial expression changed; he couldn't believe it. I stood on the other side of the counter with the exact same facial expression since I was still in complete disbelief myself.

I showed him her obituary and he could not retain that she was gone. I carried it along with me for the first two years after her death. He began to ask me 'was she sick?' and I explained to him, "no, it was SIDS". His next few words completely changed the course of grieving. He said, "You didn't have her covered up that night did you?" I said, "Of course I did, Bailey needed some sort of blanket over her as she slept. Just for comfort." He said, "No! You are not supposed to cover your baby at night, they are supposed to be in the bed with nothing". "It wasn't covering her head, just her body", I said. He then replied, "No, that can cause overheating and suffocation". I ended the conversation rather quickly after that and I rushed to the car and I balled out crying. I didn't care who saw me, I just cried out to the Lord. "Why would someone ever say that?" She was my baby and I know how and what she needed to sleep comfortably. I would never in this life time or the next put my baby in a hazardous situation. Although I knew that the jeweler's culture and practices were different, I retained the words he spoke to me in my heart. He didn't mean any harm but he planted a seed that Satan watered.

As the old saying goes "Eat the fish and throw away the bone." When you're sharing your story, most people will have an opinion and their own personal interpretation on why and how things happened. It will drive you crazy, if you let it. Take in the encouragement (fish) spit out their personal thoughts and opinions (the bone). *You must look to God and His word for your healing. Family and friends sometimes tend to lean to their own understanding when the Bible is clear in Proverbs 3:5 (ESV) "Trust in the Lord with all your heart and do not lean on your own understanding."*

RESENTMENT

I resented my understanding of faith at that time, but I mostly resented myself. The reason I struggled with my faith is because I was always taught the ask, believe and receive doctrine. You know the scriptures that we pray when we want something. The "nevertheless thy will be done" didn't quite stay with me that day. I also thought that because I was living in the way God called me to live that I would somehow be exempt from this type of loss and heart-break from the death of a child. (It was pride). I thought on all the things that I did not do and compared myself to others who lived a way worse life than I did when it came to the standards of the Bible. I just didn't get it. I resented the fact that for the rest of my life I would have to explain that my daughter died in her sleep from a diagnosis that even the doctors didn't fully understand. I had to live with the fact that there is a list of things to do and don't do. For a completely healthy baby to just stop breathing was beyond me and the more I prayed the more the Lord allowed me to understand just how far above His thinking is from ours. Even if there was a reason, I still would not have grasped the death. All of it hurt and it sucked more and more every day. Each day I woke up without Bailey, without understanding and without a perfect answer, the more confused I became. I was going through life, with a game of Scrabble playing in my mind almost constantly. I was trying to find the right words to put with every part of my new reality and I was constantly trying to fit the puzzle pieces of my new normal in its new spot. It was unending confusion.

Finally, I resented prayer. Prayer? Yes, prayer. It's because I began to question the Lord and ask him, "What is the purpose of us praying if you are going to do what you want in our life anyway?" It was a very sincere question that I had for him. I didn't understand anything anymore. The enemy was playing this game in my mind. He would say things like "God never answers your prayers. Remember you were in pain from a bad tooth and you kept praying that God would ease it and he didn't. Or, you have been praying for many years for God to change Greg but he didn't. See, prayers are pointless. God will do what he wants so there is no need for prayer." These thoughts ran through my mind constantly. I was in a low place so I dwelled on them. My mom spoke to my heart one day about the importance of praying no matter what. She reminded me of the scripture that we are to pray without ceasing. Luke 18:1 (ESV). She was right, prayer was all I had. So, I prayed, wept, believed and prayed some more leaning on everything my Bible had taught me over the years. Even though on the day my family and I needed him the most, He had seemed to turn a deaf ear and not answer. I still had to trust Him and not let the resentment from my grief question what He allowed.

We are never to compare our life to someone else's when we are faced with trials, this only brings on more resentment. Not only does it put you in God's position but it reflects the pride that is in your own heart. None of us are deserving of anything; not even our own breath. God is always good and always faithful to us and He always answers our prayers.

SIN SEARCH

I began an extensive sin search over my life. I started thinking on all the wrong I had ever done in my life. Not only did I have a game of scrabble going on in my mind, I also added a detective game. It was the enemy's perfect plan. He knew that the more I condemned myself, the further away from God I would drift. Maybe I shouldn't have gotten pregnant outside of wedlock? Maybe it was because I didn't follow my first mind the day my little sister was shot and paralyzed. Something told me "don't drive out there", but I went anyway. I literally went up and down a list of all my wrongs until all I wanted to do was bury myself under a pit of guilt.

By this time, I was in the darkest deepest pit of my life. Nothing mattered to me anymore. Surely, I was being punished by God. I didn't pray and when I did it was short prayers of me thanking him for giving me another day. Others would pray for me and I would even go up to get prayer during church but for myself, I couldn't utter a complete sentence to God.

I thank God for His grace, His grace that covered me during that rough stage. Only a loving God can do that for me. I was so broken and so out of touch with God but in His eyes, I was healed and loved. All those days and nights I cried, God was right there with a bottle collecting my tears. He did not allow not one of my tears to hit my pillow, the ground or anywhere else outside of His bottle. Although I couldn't see life without my sweet Bailey, the Lord had already given me purpose and

He knew exactly where I would be in every moment, in every stage and there was not one second that He was not with me. For that, I am forever grateful. Although I was in a pit, God sat with me and though it looked dark and dreary, there was so much light in those moments.

Looking back, I know that my heart, tears and thoughts prayed and cried out to the Lord, when my lips were too broken to speak.

If you ever find yourself searching high and low for a sin that you've committed against God that may have allowed some trouble in your life, end it now. This personal investigation of yours will lead you nowhere. True enough, some situations we find ourselves in are from choices we've made but when it comes to life and death, God and God alone has control over our birth and death date. We live in a fallen world and trouble is inevitable. So is death.

More than anything, be grateful. I am forever grateful that the Lord allowed His grace to cover my life so that I could retain and trust his word long enough until my heart could grasp it. Once my heart grasped it, I was then able to grab hold of hope and hope was then able to catch up with my faith in who God was and had proved Himself to be.

SHAME

Shame is another phase in grief that weighs heavy on the hearts of families after the loss of a child. Regret attaches itself to **shame** and they both dwell in your heart together. It is important that you know and retain in your heart that there is absolutely nothing you could have done differently that would have changed the outcome of your child or loved one passing away.

As I stated before, but it is so important that I repeat it, God is sovereign. There is absolutely nothing that comes to us that has not first left God's hands. He is in total and complete control of our life. No matter how Satan tries to plague your mind with all the *what ifs*, and *could haves* and *should haves*, the outcome would have still been the same. God is in control of time. Job 14:5 NLT says, "You have decided the length of our lives. You know how many months we will live, and we are not given a minute longer."

That means, our days were numbered, long before we were created. Once you realize this, you can detach the shame from the loss.

I believe the shame that comes along with infant loss is that we often think that others may think of us as bad parents or that maybe we didn't look after our baby close enough. The other part to that involves us believing that we are somehow reaping what we have sown.

Maybe you have had an abortion before and when your baby died, you immediately thought that surely this is your "karma" *(sin searching)*. Maybe you read the scripture in Galatians that talks about sowing and reaping. I don't know your reason for shame or regret, but what I do want you to know is that God (*although he isn't always pleased with our decisions*) would never blame us or inflict such a pain on us when we have repented and turned away from sin. This is something that I had to learn on my journey.

I pray that you release any guilt, shame or regret that you have to Jesus and allow Him to comfort and heal you, as only He can. Whenever those thoughts wash over you, you can read the scripture listed above and comfort your heart with these. "God knew this day would come long before I did and this is just His will."

> *If you are living a life of shame or regret, I encourage you to give it to God. We cannot go back in time and redo our past. The good news is we have a great future ahead and the word of God says in Jeremiah 29:11 KJV "For I know the thoughts that I think toward you, saith the Lord, thoughts of peace, and not of evil, to give you an expected end."*

FEAR

Fear was something that I struggled with up until last year, unbeknownst to me. In the beginning, I struggled with watching others sleep, especially babies. Whenever I would baby sit, I would check their respirations constantly. One night, I was so exhausted from getting up every few hours to check on my god son that I cried out to the Lord to deliver me. Satan had used Bailey's death to torment my mind with the fear of someone else not waking up in my home long enough and I refused to allow him to do it any longer. The thoughts still try to creep into my mind whenever my nieces or nephews come over but it is no longer a fear. Subtly, I had this fear of sharing advice with other moms who had questions about their newborn. I would think that other moms would believe my advice was not valid because I had lost Bailey. I can't fully describe why I felt this way but thank God, He freed me from those thoughts as well. I believe that in some way it was self-condemnation and that it was rooted in fear. The other side of fear that I was dealing with was not obvious to me because it was more of a mental battle. The thoughts of being afraid to make a wrong decision and me ending up out of God's will frightened me. I was so fearful of making a mistake that I would make up my mind not to decide in some cases, which still counts as making a decision. I would pray and cry out to God, "Lord, please show me which direction to take or what you want me to do in this situation". Fear ruled me. I would often think of him punishing me for not getting it right and this affected me greatly. July 13th, 2017, I penned this note:

"Fear has many manifestations. Meaning, you may be totally freed and fearless in one area but

it can be very present in other areas. Today I
reached out to someone to ask about one thing
and after a few short messages, she mentioned
that she too had lost a child. As the conversation
went on, I told her how fearful I am when it
comes to making decisions. I began to really
examine my ways. It's so crazy because I didn't
realize the root of this fear until today. Wow. It
is from Bailey's death."

The enemy knows how to keep you trapped.
Did you know that one tragedy can change your
entire perspective on decision making?

I realized that fear held me captive. I fell to my knees and asked the Lord to forgive me. I asked that He order my steps and that He give me the faith to make decisions trusting that He will get me to my destiny safely. I prayed that Bailey's death and the fear that was attached to it no longer controlled me. I knew that the root of this fear was the fact that I had not fully accepted God's love, which leads me to my final stage.

ACCEPTING GOD'S LOVE

Accepting God's love for me was one of the hardest truths for me to retain. I have stated this over and over I know but it warrants being repeated. We can know the truth, we can recite it, we can pray it and we can speak it into the lives of others. But the true test is hanging on to God's love when you are hurting. The true test is resting in that love when you don't feel it physically. The greatest test is trusting His love even when you feel as though He is chastising you. I believe that I struggled with this based on my view of how others loved and accepted me. When I did not measure up to their standards or please them in a way that they thought I should, they reneged on their love and their commitment to me. I believe I compared Christ's acceptance of me to the acceptance of humans. I had to remind myself that God loves and accepts me. God loves and accepts you. He doesn't agree with or accept our mess but He is gracious to us. He forgives and He is constantly leading us in the right direction. You don't have to live in fear that God is ready to judge you and take you to hell as soon as you make a mistake. No, that is a lie from Satan. God does discipline us when we rebel but it is all out of love. Even in His discipline, He is still loving on us.

God will never change His thoughts towards you, even when you mess up. The powerful thing about God is that He knew every mistake that you would ever make and He still sent His son Jesus to die for you. He thought you were worth saving and if there was no other human being on earth besides you, Jesus would have still gone to the cross on your behalf. His blood covers past, present and future mistakes and contrary to how others have loved you, God's love is never-ending. I encourage you to accept his love and accept that even in your grief His love is with you. You have no reason to Fear.

Chapter 9

TRUSTING GOD WHEN YOU CAN'T TRACE HIM

TRUST. It took a while for me to get to this stage of trusting and believing God's heart and His permissive will even when I can't trace his heart. But I finally did and boy was a weight lifted off me. God is sovereign. That means that there is absolutely nothing that happens to us that doesn't first go through Him. When I fully understood this, that in itself took a load of "What if's" off my heart. Although I didn't fully understand the 'why', I knew that God was still in control of the 'when' and the 'how'. I also knew that it was time to reflect on the infamous question, "What does God want me to learn and do in this tragedy?" Death takes control away from you and opens your eyes to how we take life for granted. We don't realize just how important it is to breathe on this side, but death reminds us of this truth. I believe that is another component of grief that adds to your sorrow. Human beings relish over the idea of being in control. We like to control our finances, where we go, what we eat, how we spend God's time.

If we are honest, we would like to control our very lives and the manner and time in which we die. But life and death are the very things that we don't have control over. I wrestled with that, day in and day out. I thought, "if the Lord just came in and allowed her to die unexpectedly, what else will He take?" Nothing was safe anymore. Some nights I was afraid to fall asleep because I knew I had no control over waking up. What if the Lord decided that my purpose was finished and that He needed me to be with Him? I began to pray and ask the Lord to help me with the issues that I had with this fear. I always talked about trusting God, now it was really time to let go and trust Him with every fiber of my being. It is hard to trust God when you've already been so accustomed to planning and figuring out your life. There have been countless testimonies of God showing His people little bits and pieces of their lives, even the most spiritual Christians only know "in part". As I stated before, I knew the Lord was preparing me for something, I just didn't know what it was. I sometimes wish I would have paid closer attention to the Lord and the signs He gave me leading up to Bailey's death. God often does that with us. He will give us a word before we go into a tough season.

Looking back, had He revealed that my daughter would leave me, there is no way I could have handled that. I am grateful once again that He holds the position of God and chose to do things the way He did. My mom began to remind me of so many things that folks had said to me during my pregnancy. I remember my pastor praying for me, saying,

"Can God trust you with trouble?" He asked me this three times one Sunday as I stood in line for prayer. This was something that I had completely forgotten about. Again, that is an example of the 'living life forward but understanding it backwards' analogy. I had trouble in my life but shortly after he asked that, she passed away.

The biggest part of trust is letting go of the need to understand. We can weave our minds into a ball of confusion when we try and figure out why God allows tough circumstances in our life. The biggest misconception of pain and tough seasons is that in those seasons we feel as though things will never change. Or how things are is how they will always be. I am learning every day that with every trial and heart-break that God has allowed in my life, it has never been to hurt me but to help me to grow and evolve with Him. I use the analogy of our adversity being a bridge to get us to the other side. The other side of us getting to know ourselves and God in a deeper way. This bridge is not just in death but in any situation. Financial problems, divorce, friendships that suddenly end, etc. We as human beings like to feel that we have our life under control or that we can predict what a certain outcome will be. That is where we go wrong because we can't. From one moment to the next, we don't know what the Lord will allow to hit our life.

As I mentioned before, Bailey's death wasn't the only thing I was dealing with at the time. After her death, I didn't return to work right away so financially, I was pressed. I maxed out my savings and credit cards during that time.

Then, the worst blow was watching as my children tried to navigate through their emotions of death and losing their little sister at such a young age. Some nights, they would be afraid to fall asleep as well because they didn't know if the Lord would allow them to die. Other moments, they would just cry and ask why did she have to die. It was the hardest thing ever. As a parent, even when you don't fully understand you can rationalize in your mind and come to some sort of conclusion that will help you process it all but as a kid, they had nothing. Nothing but "She is in heaven now with Jesus". I would quote scriptures and write them on our chalk board but they didn't grasp the power of God's word. How could they understand that and still trust that Jesus was loving?

I prayed daily for my children, I prayed that God would work in their life and give them a purpose in life that far exceeded mine. I had dealt with a lot as a child with not having a father and living with a verbally abusive step dad, but I couldn't ever compare my childhood to theirs. It sucked. Some days when they would walk past me, I would turn away or look down just so I didn't have to look at their face. I could see the hurt plastered over their faces and I knew that all they wanted was to see or hold their baby sister. I prayed that they didn't have any regrets. Like wishing they had held her longer or checked on her that night. I knew I had plenty but I didn't want them to think for one moment that maybe they should have done anything differently in Bailey's four-months of living. I kept trusting that things would get easier.

Once I was trying to take a nap and I remember asking Alasijah to look after Bailey until I got up. She did but I knew she was trying to play her game. After about fifteen minutes, I heard her huffing and puffing as Bailey fussed a little. I am sure she wanted to be held. I thought back on moments like that and prayed that those moments didn't come to *her* mind. I had conversations with them concerning death and how they feel about it. Their answers varied but one thing was clear; they did not understand why it happened to Bailey. I explained that everything in life comes down to our trust and faith in God and His word. It's all we have.

If you are struggling with trusting God in your grief at this moment, I would like to offer some practical tips on how to deal with it.

1. *Don't rush the process.* As I stated before, healing from grief is a journey. It takes time to get to a place where you find the balance of still missing your baby but not allowing that emotion to control your life. You have to get through each moment, rather than focusing on tomorrow, next month or next year. I learned that God gives us grace and mercy for each day on purpose. Lamentation 3:22 NLT says, "*Great is His faithfulness; His mercies begin afresh each morning*". You can't take today's grace into tomorrow and you can't gather your future grace to use today. All of the ups and downs are

normal and in order to find balance in your day, you must trust the process and the grace that God has bestowed for the day.

2. *Daily Positive affirmation.* Renewing your mind is an important principle. You must wake up and affirm yourself with God's truth. I used to look in the mirror and say things like, "You will be alright. God has a purpose in all of this. You are healed. God is in full control. You are beautiful. Your life is worth living. God is at work. The teacher is always quiet during the test but your teacher (Holy Spirit) is with you. You will get through this. One day this pain won't hurt so bad. Trust the process." I had to remind myself of these truths as well as Bible verses daily. I wrote them on sticky tabs and stuck them all around my house in places like my headboard, mirrors, I even wrote them on my chalk board. I kept them in common places and used them as reminders.

3. *Don't suffer in silence.* Share your pain with those who are close to you and who you know are praying for you. One of the worst things you can do while grieving is secluding yourself from the ones that you know love you. The psalmist David was struggling when he didn't share his truth and this is what he said in Psalms 32:3 (ESV) *"For when I kept silent, my bones wasted away through my groaning all day long."* He understood that silence wrecked him more mentally and emotionally. It

is important that you don't allow the loneliness you feel to keep you stuck in the bed all day. Every conversation, every prayer, every laugh and every tear matters in this season of healing. At the time, it may feel like no one understands and that's ok, they don't. That does not mean that you ought to shut the door to help.

4. *Journaling.* I cannot describe how putting pen to paper during my heavy stages of grief helped shift my perspective. Journaling is therapeutic. Sometimes it's difficult to verbally express how you feel but when you write, with every stroke of your pen you will release pain and the thoughts that tormented your mind. I also shared my fears and all of my hopes in my journal. I looked back each month on my writing and saw the progress. I saw how God was intricately involved in each day and it brought great comfort to my heart. I also noticed how God was answering questions that I had hidden in my heart about myself and my grief as well as prayers that I was too embarrassed to speak. I truly believe journaling changed my life.

5. *Shut out comparison.* It is never good to compare your grief journey, it only drives a wedge between what God is doing in your life. Sometimes you can look at the strength that others appear to have and wish that you were like them. These thoughts are not of God. I learned this the hard way. I almost missed out on what God wanted to do through my life by dwelling and

almost mimicking someone else's grief journey. God's plan and process for healing is different for each journey.

6. *Release.* You must release regret, shame, unforgiveness, and self-condemnation. Give all those ill feelings to God. You win a race by running forward not looking backwards. You can't change the past, instead use the lessons you've learned to help someone else. You must release these thoughts as often as they appear.

7. *Trust God.* I know I expounded on this earlier but this point is important. Even when you don't understand, trust God.

8. *Daily devotion.* Honestly this should be at the top of the list but it's so important that you set aside time each day to read the Bible, pray and share your heart with God. I don't care if you have to sit in the closet or your bathroom floor, devote some quiet time to God. Sit in His presence and ask Him to give you a verse to meditate on for the day and ask that He lead and guide your day. If you believe the Lord is pressing something on your heart, write it down in your journal. Devoting time to God is important and it helps redirect your thoughts away from your situation and onto God and His plan. Devotion is a form of worship and it is vital nourishment to your mind, body and soul. Balancing life and grief can be tough but when you devote time to God, He will see to it that your day is "God speed".

Trusting God when you can't trace Him is one of the hardest things to do, I understand. But when you are faced with pain, it's your only option.

Chapter 10

TRUE HEALING

The journey to healing is a long and extensive one, but it is attainable. I once was asked if I had any recommendations for a book to help a grieving mom heal. I had seen several women share how books helped them better understand what they are feeling. For me, it was the total opposite. I could not look to anyone else's experience but I had to look to God and His word for the truth. Healing comes from the truth of God's word. God was the one that allowed this, so for me, it was Him and only Him that I needed to look to. Don't get me wrong. Books are great, I mean, I am writing one. But during my dark days, I had to know what God's word said about my grief before I could look to someone else's experience. As I live out each day, one thing I noticed is that to get through life after loss, you must rely wholly on Jesus Christ, His word, prayer, Godly counsel and community. There is absolutely no way I could get through a day without falling to my knees and asking the Lord for His strength, wisdom and grace. God gives us grace daily.

If you don't trust God daily, you can end up on a slippery path back down to the pits. It is so easy to fall back into that pit of despair. The battle in your mind is a real one and if you are not guarding your heart, Satan will infiltrate it with all kind of lies. He is the accuser of the brethren, meaning he loves to dig up dirt from your past to remind you of times when you failed God. The times when you failed yourself. There were several nights where I cried from my decisions in the past. I thought if I had not had sex out of wedlock then maybe I would not be experiencing this pain from adultery. It was thoughts like this which would slow down my progress and push me back down. I would fight back by saying, "No, God forgave me and He loves me", but the accusations kept coming until I felt like I had no fight left. Sometimes I preferred to cry myself to sleep hoping that tomorrow I could win the battle in my mind. I once wrote this on social media...

> *Grief has a way of reappearing in a more devastating way when other areas of our life seem to be falling apart.*
>
> *I remember months after Bailey passed when I was on a semi good path of healing. I had accepted the fact that she was now in heaven and never returning. It was hard but it was under control. Then, other close relationships began to fall apart. I remember sitting in the room weeping about Bailey all over again, digging her*

up just to grieve her when really my hurt was because of other situations.

Your mind is a real battlefield. You conquer your thoughts but the moment another attack comes in we tend to go dig up all that we were hurt about in the past and mourn those. "I wish I could of and should of" begin to drown our mind and before you know it, you are thinking on your life from stages as early as when you were a kid.

It is so important that we guard our hearts and minds from these attacks. Yes, you will hurt when someone else wrongs you and that's ok, but don't go digging up the past and dwelling on that too. It only hurts more.

I encourage you to reach for a journal and write about the things that are hurting your heart as well as pray instead of grabbing the "mental shovel" to dig in your past.

God sees and knows everything and He has said time and time again how the battles that we fight are not ours. We must be more intentional about trusting God with our hurt and pain. It's the only way we can stay in a healthy place mentally.

Put the shovel away!

I wrote this because I finally understood that the true battle that we are all fighting is in our mind. Once I was able to take hold of my thoughts and think on what I knew to be true and what God's word said about my life, true healing began. You see, that's the medicine to all our issues in life. God's word is the purest form of hope that has ever been recorded. Folks have written books on meditation, self-help guides but none of that appealed to me. The Bible says in Psalms 147:3 ESV *"He heals the brokenhearted and binds up their wounds"*. I was wounded. I was wounded badly. The scars that were dormant in my heart stemmed from a young age. I never fully recovered from things that were said and done to me in the past and grief added to those wounds. As I began to soak in God's love for me, everything started to make sense. My thought patterns began to shift, so did my actions and I came face to face with my own truth.

RUG IN OUR HEART

I always say that we women do a fine job in "sweeping things under the rug". I believe that we all have a rug in our heart that has accumulated a number of hurtful things from our past. When you're on the journey to true healing, God will lift that rug and dig up everything that you had buried; all your pain, mistakes, the rejection, betrayal, the inadequacies and failures. He will pull those emotions and hurts out one by one and call for you to confront it. When you bring light to the dark areas of your heart, you'll begin to walk in freedom. You are to trust that God will toss your shortcomings into the sea of forgetfulness. The memory may still be there but He removes the pain from your heart.

It is important that we acknowledge our hurt. We go through life saying, "oh I'm okay, I'm alright" when we know we're not. Yes, it is easier to hide behind "I'm ok" than to express how you truly feel but it's not healthy. God was digging deep within me during this stage because I needed to know and experience true healing. Not just from grief, but from the pain of life. Bitterness surfaced, unforgiveness surfaced, unbelief, low self-esteem, low self-worth, co-dependency (*relying on others for fulfillment over God*) and pride all rose up in me. I had to repent for all these issues and allow God to get to the root of them. God is still at work in me but none of these characteristics would have surfaced had I not humbled my heart during my season of grief. Again, this is God rebuilding me for His glory.

HOW ARE YOU SO STRONG?

I get asked often, "how are you so strong". People want to understand why my posts are always encouraging and never down. My answer is always simply, 'I am not'. I am dust. It is God who gives me the grace to keep going. I have many days where I ride around and just cry. I have days when I am confused and wonder if I am in God's will. In those moments,

I allow myself to feel what I feel, but I don't allow it to dictate my life. The only road map I follow is truth. On the days when I am overwhelmed, I try and think on truth. What does God say about my circumstances? What does God say about death and seeing Bailey again? What does God say about my trouble?

> *Many are the afflictions of the righteous: but the LORD delivereth him out of them all.* Psalms 34:19 KJV

From this scripture I understand that I will be afflicted, I will hurt in this life, I may encounter sickness and even death of other family members. But God, He promised to deliver. You see, this is the principle behind truth. It is believing and clinging to what God says about you in His word and not what you see. Truth is trusting the invisible while walking through the visible. That is where my strength lies. That is where your strength is as well. Prayer renews your mind and allows you to focus on what's to come versus what is. That's the beauty in our pain. All of it is for a purpose. I am the first to say that I am weak. But in God, I am mightier than Goliath and not only does He give me mercy daily, but He also renews my strength. I rely wholly on God, His word, prayer and Godly counsel. In closing, all of me points back to the one who created me. My God, Yahweh

MY JOURNEY TO HEALING

If I can sum up the steps God took me through, it would be this list below. I ask that you read them and focus not so much on the steps but on the principles in each step.

Before I jump into this list, I would like to first acknowledge the importance of forgiveness. Before you can embark on the journey of healing, you must first forgive yourself. I ask that you search your heart. Search those secrets and regrets that no one knows about except you and God. Forgiveness is key because it allows the Lord to soften those spaces in our hearts that have hardened over time. If you have experienced rejection, death, loneliness, abuse etc. and you feel deep down in your heart that part of it is your fault, pause right now and release it. Give it all to God. You don't need to carry the weight of not forgiving yourself or your offenders any longer.

God has forgiven you now you forgive you. This step opens the door for True healing.

- My **first** point would be I prayed and repented. Not just any old prayer but a long and agonizing honest, prayer. I told the Lord how much of a wreck I was and that I knew that if He didn't help me, I couldn't be helped. I repented meaning I turned away from the ways and thoughts that were not like God.

- **Secondly,** I began to share my truth with myself and others. I shared how hurtful it was to wake up each day, heartbroken and still have to get through life. Transparency is key.

- **Thirdly,** I poured into others. Encouraging them in my pain, helped heal me. While sharing some words of hope, God would allow those words to flow out my mouth to other's hearts and then use those same words to ricochet, driving that truth right back into my own heart.

- **Fourth,** I sought to know God more deeply. I wanted to understand the God who held both life and death in His hands. I believed all my life I knew God in one way but the depth of this pain was so real and so intense, I needed to know Him more intimately. I began to pray daily and read my Bible like my life depended on it. In reality, my life did depend on it.

- **Fifth,** I listened to broadcasts daily. I wish I could describe in depth how much listening to Pastors (**Dr. Charles Stanley, Paul Sheppard, Tony Evans, June Hunt, John Macarthur, and David Jeremiah**, just to name a few) completely changed my life and my view on all the things I had been through. Many days I would just weep listening as they described how God worked in their lives. I truly believe if I had not found them when I did, the pit that I had made my home would have been a longer resting place for me. I no longer had a desire to watch TV or any other nonproductive thing. I just wanted to listen, read the word and pray for myself and the other hearts that suffered from heart break.

- **Sixth**, I found purpose. I began to look at the gifts and talents that the Lord gave to me and I knew that my purpose on earth was far greater than what my mind could fathom. I learned first-hand that purpose is truly found through pain. This was one of the greatest revelations of my life. As I looked over biblical figures like Joseph, Moses, Ruth & Naomi, David and Paul just to name a few, I saw how God used everything that they went through to get them to their destiny. Their story was uniquely crafted, they suffered and overcame and in the end, God was glorified.

- **Seventh**, I surrendered. I stopped trying to live life in the way that I had planned it, but instead I gave everything over to God. It's like I used a pencil and wrote out everything I ever dreamed of doing. Then I handed the pencil to God and allowed him to erase it all and write His desires on my heart.

- **Eighth**, I began to listen closely to God's instructions and I obeyed. Obedience was the key to my healing. I know you may wonder how and why that would be important. Part of my healing involved apologizing to others and correcting offenses that I did. One instance I will never forget is the day God led me to go and apologize to Greg. I remember thinking, "but Lord, he committed adultery, he hurt me". In those moments, it wasn't about what he did, it was about me releasing myself from the emotional pain. Grief in your heart often is intensified when others have hurt you. All those wounds live in the same place, spreading and growing like organisms as long as you harbor them there and don't deal with them. So, I did it. I didn't receive the response I expected but walking away, I felt so free. It's like the Lord patched that space up immediately and my shattered heart continued to mend.

- **Ninth**, I began to look deeper into my own heart and ways. You never know how many negative and bad habits you have internally until you begin to heal and the Lord shines a light on those places. Listen, I was a wretch undone. I was so insecure, filled with pride (unbeknownst to me). I felt as though if I hid behind religion I deserved nothing but good. I was surprised at some of my recordings after Bailey passed away. I would tell the Lord all the things I didn't do and ask, "so why did He allow this." I was like that Pharisee who stood and prayed in the temple while the tax collector bowed his head. I am embarrassed that I thought so highly of my works. I really wasn't trusting in God, I was trusting in good works and God exposed all of that. I was filled with so much remorse. I began to pray for and understand people and the sin that they struggled with. I was no longer upset with the folks who hurt me deeply but I now had a deep compassion for them. I understood my need for compassion and mercy and it humbled me in a way that is indescribable.

- **Tenth**, I simply trusted God. I never really trusted God as much as I thought I did. Once I realized that and that I am in control of nothing, it changed my perspective on trust. It changed my perspective on life. God is sovereign. He has ruled and reigned since the beginning of time. His thoughts are not our thoughts and His ways are not our ways. God never intended for life to be as hard as it is, especially when we look at death, disease, natural disasters, violence, etc. These things are occurring because of the fall of man. The truth is, we will have trouble until Jesus returns. The good news is that His promises are true and He promised to never leave us or forsake us. I cannot function one second without God. I need him more than words can express. When the weight of the world weighs me down and I am pressed with trouble on every side, I can look to heaven and know that as the tears flow from my tear ducts that God is with me. That is ultimately what trust is. It is trusting God in the crucible of times even when you can't trace him. When you fully trust, you can fully heal.

Then it happened....

I finally began to feel a shift in my heart. Other areas in my life had fallen completely apart but it did not matter. My faith was unshaken. I knew that if God was working this work of healing in my heart, nothing could lead me back into that slump of depression. I had buried my daughter therefore nothing else could break me as that did.

I was becoming a new person. I understood my value in Christ and it was the most amazing discovery of all my years of living. I fell deeply in love with God and got to a place where it didn't matter what He allowed, I knew that He loved me. I knew that I would never have to face life alone. I knew that God had been with me every step of every day and there was never a time where He was not in control. This brought me peace. It brought me joy. It's almost as if I began to understand the why in a lot of things that had occurred in my life. I found myself going back to situations and understanding why God allowed the hurt and why He blocked me from things that would have ultimately been my demise.

You see, pain drives you to your knees. It is a tool that humbles even the lowly. I would think on Job and feel so badly for him. Although I hadn't experienced nearly as much as he did, I know the pain of trying to live right yet finding yourself in the midst of a storm that you question why you were even born.

When you are in the thick of your suffering, God seems so far away. You know that He is close and carrying you because there is no way you could be making it without Him, yet the pain of it all is so intense you actually feel the ache in your heart. It's a very real and physical ache that makes you question if you are needing medical assistance. No seriously! I know that I laid down many nights wondering if I would need to go to the ER because I feared that the pain of life would cause my heart to stop beating.

I know this to be true, on those nights when the tears fell silently, that God was right there with me, comforting and healing my heart all at the same time. Jesus is a healer. He heals our wounds from both the past and future. God always has a plan in a plan but you must trust him. You must hang on to the hope that He is working something far greater than your eyes could see.

If you are struggling with finding true healing and you have not accepted Jesus Christ as your Lord and savior, first start there. The good news is that God sent his only son Jesus Christ to die on the cross for your sins. He suffered a horrible death with YOU in mind. Three days later He rose with Victory, Power and the keys to both death and life. He wants to give you that life today so I ask that you pray and ask him to forgive you of your sins and that He would come into your heart. It is only through Jesus Christ that you can receive the healing that you so desperately need.

TWO PERSPECTIVES OF HEALING

There are two perspectives of healing. *Healing with God and without God.* I have seen someone lose a loved one and never recover from it. I watched as they lost hope, faith and their morals because they could not cope with the pain. In most cases, they blamed God instead of trusting His will.

Life is too difficult for anyone to try and navigate without God. Adding grief to our troubled life only makes things worse. We need an anchor. We need Jesus Christ. Our faith in Jesus and what he accomplished on the cross gives us all hope in the seasons when we require healing. Without Him, there is no solid foundation.

We can't rely on alcohol because when the buzz goes down so does our escape. We can't trust in drugs to get us through because when the high goes down it will take us down with it. We can't rely on friends to talk us through because when life gets busy for them they will not be there for us.

I said all that to say, Jesus is your only constant. Vices are fickle, and they can never give you the true healing you need. Yes, they may take your thoughts away from your reality but when the highs wear off, you must face reality and your hurt.

A person who grieves with God will have a perspective on healing. Although they hurt and they don't understand the why, there is this flicker of hope that is in their soul that keeps them going on the days that they want to give up. It's like a fire that is shut up in their bones that says, God has a plan. Even when they feel down, the Holy Spirit reminds them of a scripture or some comforting words to confirm that God is still at work in their life.

So, grieving with God is always the best way. I say this often, I would rather have bad days with God then good days without Him. I mean that from the bottom of my heart! His presence is so powerful and He is the comforter of all comforters. I admonish you to set your foundation on Jesus Christ. It is in him and him alone that true healing emerges. By His stripes, you are healed. If you have sought healing without God, it is not too late to turn around. Pray and ask God to help you understand how much you need Him in this process and begin again.

AS I CLOSE THIS CHAPTER,

You have heard how God turned things around for me but maybe you are wondering if and how this may apply to you. You may feel like I once did, hopeless. Even after reading the different stages He walked me through, you may feel as though none of this has been working or will work for you. I want to reassure you that it can and it will. You are no different than I am. True healing comes down to having a willing heart and learning to trust God. There is no way around healing of grief outside of simply trusting God with your loved one and the future of your life. I don't believe that I had to get as low as rock bottom in the way that I did. The blessing in it all is that *God used that low place to reveal to me that He was the rock at the bottom.*

So, is there any way that your heart can be mended after losing a child? Yes. Can you ever fully recover? Yes. The answer is Yes, absolutely you can. The choice is left up to you. You can look at your loss as if God has taken away something essential in your life or you can trust that even in death, God is still good.

I would like to say a prayer with you.

> Lord, first we thank you for this day, we thank you for the very air that we are breathing. This is a hard task, believing that you will bind our brokenness and heal our wounds. Tears flow as we ask. We believe in your son Jesus Christ and we believe that He died for our sins. We believe that He died so that we may experience true healing and we ask that you heal our hearts right now in Jesus name. Lord, when the lights go down and everyone is asleep, I lay awake as tears flood my pillow because my heart is so overwhelmed with grief. I loved my love one, and I never imagined saying goodbye so soon. But you knew this day would come so I ask that you comfort me even now. Your word says that when

I walk through the fire, I shall not be burned. Lord I am in the fire and it feels as though it is consuming me. I need you, I need you now more than ever. Please heal me. Please lead me in the way that I should go. Change my thoughts. Change the way I view death. I know that we are separated now but give me the reassurance that I will see my baby again. I know it is beautiful in heaven, and that there is no pain nor suffering. Help me to trust in your perfect will and continue to remind me that all things will work together for my good. Help me to trust that even in this pain, I know that you love me and that you have a purpose for my life. In Jesus name I pray, Amen.

Chapter 11

GRACE FOR THE JOURNEY

Sometimes we as parents are afraid to truly move on. We want to, but fear grips us. We are afraid to say that we are having a good day or that we are actually getting better. Sometimes we feel as if those very words are banned from our vocabulary. I found it very hard to say that I was having a good day. I never wanted anyone to think that I had fully gotten over the death of Bailey, but then I didn't want anyone to think that I was depressed either. Whenever you say, "good day" it's not as if it still doesn't hurt, it just means that instead of breaking down five times, today you cried once or maybe you thought of your loved one and smiled because of the memories. I sometimes see my family grieving and I am at peace, but then I feel badly because they are weeping. Then, on other occasions, if no one mentions her name, I feel sad, thinking that they have forgotten about her. These feelings are normal and are all part of the wave of grief.

I would encourage anyone who is finally starting to see a glimpse of light at the end of the tunnel, to be honest. If you are healing and you know that the Lord is giving you peace, rest in that. Don't try and explain why you are not as emotional as you were two days ago. We all heal differently, we deal with grief and hurt in unique ways. It may take someone five weeks to heal from something and take another person five months. I can sit down and describe how I feel to ten different women and the only thing we would agree on is that it hurt. Building the description on how bad it hurt is unique to each heart. No two hearts are the same. Grief is relative. My journey will not look like yours and that is ok. Trust where you are in the process but most of all trust the Grace that He has given you for your journey. His Grace in His time is the supernatural power that you need internally to get you to your next phase in life.

HEART CHECKS

Heart checks are necessary. We must continue to ask the Lord to search our hearts and minds for any underlying bitterness, anger, self-un-forgiveness, regret, and shame. During your different stages of grief, the pain that you feel after the loss can water those other seeds and before you know it, you have all sorts of unhealthy feelings growing inside your heart. Imagine that you're sitting at home reflecting on how much you miss your child, then that reflection leads to you thinking about past hurts. Your mind takes you on an adventure and you think "nothing good ever happens to me" or "it seems as if I'm under a curse, everyone around me either dies or get sick". Before you know it, you'll begin to feel even more depressed because you've never truly healed and allowed the Lord to pluck those negative seeds out. My mind can travel back to places I never want to visit. In those times, when every thought seems to bring me lower, I pull out my Bible and search for verses about God's love and forgiveness. I think on the scripture in Philippians 4:8 ESV *"Finally, brothers, whatever is true, whatever is honorable, whatever is just, whatever is pure, whatever is lovely, whatever is commendable, if there is any excellence, if there is anything worthy of praise, think about these things."*

I do this because I don't want anything that happened to me in my past to control my future. More than anything, I can take my pain and experiences and use my story to encourage someone else. Learn from your hurt, don't water those negative seeds and please don't bury it. At the first sight of rain (trouble) in your life, every emotion that you buried will sprout up again.

DEATH IS A TEACHER

Death teaches you valuable lessons that can only be learned in death. It was in Bailey's death that I learned how to live. I learned the value of spending time and cherishing your loved ones while they're here on earth. Another lesson was learning to live in the moment. I also learned the value of trusting God when I didn't understand.

You know all these years I went through my life proclaiming how much I trusted God. But pain and grief revealed that I really didn't. I didn't know God as a father or one who would communicate with me. I knew of him. I knew the emotion of loving Him and wanting to do His will. I came to really know God late in the midnight hours, when my heart felt the constant stabbing pain of grief and heart-break that would not subside. The moment I felt the weight lift, in came another dagger that almost took me out. But God. God came in and rescued me. His loving hands lifted me out of despair and hopelessness. He affirmed me through His word and showed me infallible truths. I could have never made it this far without His saving power. I learned just how real God is and I am so glad that in those dark moments, I whispered "Yes Lord, let your will be done in and through my life. I will forever and always trust you".

I learned that God keeps His promises. I learned that He is faithful and His love never fails. People have failed me but God, He has never failed me. Oh, the tears that come to my heart when I think on that simple yet profound truth. "What if He had left me? What if He had given up on me, when I gave up on myself?" The thought of that drives me to my knees. Bailey's death was never just about me, it was about God. It was the Lord showing me how He can take the worst of broken hearts, crush it some more and still make a beautiful piece of mosaic art.

The greatest loss, the one that changed me the most, was me losing myself yet finding my true identity in Christ. The greatest lesson that I learned is that God never changed. When I went to the lowest depths from pain, He was God. When death occurred, He was God. When times were good, He was God. When times were confusing, He was still God. He has and will always remain in His position and He is and will forever be God in life and in death. The measure of grace that He continues to give daily is the perfect measure for our life's journey.

Chapter 12

LOVE REMAINS

Death takes a lot from you and it also takes a lot out of you. Two things that death cannot steal are the love we had for our baby and the memories; I believe memories can work two-fold. On one hand, when memories from your past are associated with hurt and pain caused by others even after you have forgiven them, the memory is still present and can be a very painful reminder of what you went through. *In this instance, we pray and ask God to remove them.* But the flip side of that coin is after death, memories such as pictures, personal items, and if we are lucky, videos are all we have left. *We pray that they never leave our mind because it is the stitch that keeps us connected to our loved ones.* When my heart is heavy and I'm missing my Bailey, I can stare at her picture or think on a moment and smile. I am very grateful for that. Memory is a gift from God. A gift that no amount of grief can steal away from you. Reflecting over life and the other troubles that I encountered in life, yes, those memories hurt but they are also reminders of how far I've come and I am grateful for the lessons in it all. Pain teaches us lessons, valuable lessons that can only be taught through experience. You know, I always hear others reference the poem "Foot prints in the sand" and I don't think I understood the depth of that poem until now. God has carried me for sure. I think on the weight of life and all the pressure from my marriage, children, friends, and then I think on how I made it through what seemed to be a never-ending storm. Isaiah 43:2 ESV says *" When you pass through the waters, I will be with you; and through the rivers, they shall not overwhelm you; when you walk through fire you shall not be burned, and the flame shall not consume you. "* This is a scripture that you want to keep near your heart. In every circumstance God is with you, just as He has been with me. Not only is God with you but His *love remains*. Each day God gives us grace and mercy to endure what we are to face. His *love remains* with us when we are hurting, heart-broken, financially stretched, abused, cast down, rejected and betrayed. No matter where you are, God's love is with you. It is hard for us to trust His love when we can't trace Him in our life. But you must hang on to the hope that it is the same love that is walking with you today that will be the delivering agent of your tomorrow. The Bible says this in Psalms 30:5 KJV *"...weeping may endure for a night, but joy cometh in the morning"*. Morning doesn't always mean the following day in the natural. Morning simply means the day that is set on God's timetable that says enough is enough. Your morning is when you finally see the rainbow just as the storm ends. It will be a day that you are able to reflect back to the day your heart was first struck with grief and the journey it took for you to experience true healing. You will rest in God's love that has remained with you and will until the day He calls you home.

This entire journey, the Lord has allowed me to see and understand that Bailey's death, all the pain and suffering I endured and every circumstance that I faced up unto this day, was never just about me. It was the powerful and sovereign hand of God that used pain on this earth to accomplish His purpose for His kingdom. Bailey's death isn't ruled SIDS per my conviction. ***SIDS was just a natural name put on a supernatural purpose and plan that God had.*** I laid her down but God raised her up and He took her to her eternal home. No man can explain this. No doctor can convince me of anything else because the doctor of all doctors which is Jesus Christ was ultimately in control of her life and death. The Bible says this " *Your eyes saw my unformed substance; in your book were written, every one of them, the days that were formed for me, when as yet there was none of them" Psalms 139:16* ESV. Bailey's death was not a mistake. She didn't leave too soon. God was not picking on me, and He certainly didn't look down from heaven and say, "Let's just take Bailey, Bettye can bear this." No. Her death wasn't a product of reaping what I had sown. I stand on this truth today. You see, years ago I did a thing that I had yet to share with anyone besides Greg. He was with me and I told one other friend. My family didn't even know because I was too embarrassed to share. I had an abortion after my daughter Briyah was born. I knew that it was wrong but my heart and conscious was hardened. I wasn't living for God instead I was selfishly following my flesh. I prayed and asked God to forgive me as I laid on that table to have the life in me aborted. I was going through way too much at the time and thought that if I brought another baby in my dysfunctional home, I would lose my mind. Greg was treating me horribly and I was constantly finding out about different women. It was too much. The funny thing is, looking back, God allowed the same circumstances to come back around years later (*Pregnant with Bailey while in the middle of another affair*).

Satan planted all kinds of thoughts in my mind to abort Bailey. My own reasoning was there reminding me of all my troubles as well. But I did not allow those thoughts to win. I didn't care what happened. I was determined to do what was right in God's eyes this time. Many nights after Bailey passed away, I sat and reflected on the abortion. I was reaping what I had sown and Satan and my own conscience made sure that I knew it. But it was lies. Yes, I did suffer greatly from my consequences but the suffering was more mental than anything. Sometimes your consequence is the mental reminder of what you did. But the condemning thoughts are seeds that Satan tried to plant in my mind to keep me locked away in fear. He wanted to hinder me from sharing my truth. But God reminded me that He forgave me a long time ago and though this sin happened, it can no longer hinder me or my testimony.

I am a sinner, this I know. I did not deserve God's grace, this is true too. Everything God has allowed in my life that is good, I do not deserve, yes, I know this. This is why I live so radically for God. This is why I am sold out until death. God forgave me and I do not have to live in the prison of secrets instead I can walk openly in God's Grace and mercy. I am free and the best part of all is that God's Love for me *still Remains*.

The devil may be planting these seeds or other destructive thoughts in your mind as well and my prayer is that you retain in your heart that God is and will always be in control. Your past is your past and the Bible says this:

> *He will again have compassion on us,*
> *And will subdue our iniquities.*
> *You will cast all our sins*
> *Into the depths of the sea.* Micah 7:19 ESV

Your sins were cast into the sea. Not once did God ask that we go diving to pull them up. The Lord knew in times past all my mistakes and His blood would atone for them all.

Before Bailey was formed in my womb God knew the purpose and plan He had for her life as well. He knew that she would be born two days before my birthday and would live for four months and two days. Bailey's life was filled with purpose. Despite the fact that she was a baby, I believe she knew that

she was different. She knew that she was sent here for a
heavenly purpose and that soon she would be taken up during
the night to be with her Heavenly King. Our Heavenly King.
Oh, and I long for the day that I get to meet my Savior and see
my princess. I live daily for purpose because I understand that
everything that I see with my natural eyes are temporal while
the things that I can't see are eternal. I can't see Bailey because
she is now an eternal being but someday I will. I will take off
my mortality to put on immortality and hopefully that comes
when Jesus returns. We will defeat death because the Bible has
declared it and I believe that death has already been swallowed
up. I find comfort in this verse from Isaiah 65:20 (ESV) "*No
more shall there be in it an infant who lives but a few days, or
an old man who does not fill out his days....*"

The very death, hurt, pain, mistakes and grief that the devil
tried to torment my mind with are the very things that God
used. It was all of these things which drove me down to my
knees, humbling me before almighty God. It was in her death
that I died too. I died to my own selfish desires and
comfortability and made the necessary changes to allow God
to propel my life forward. We are to forget those things that
are behind, no longer allowing them to be an excuse or
hindrance to our future. Two important decisions that I made
for my life were to file for a divorce from Greg and to divorce
my past as well. My love for Greg *still remains*. It's a love that
wants to see him saved and living for God. I pray for him daily
and although we had bad times, there were also great times

that I am forever grateful for. Greg has a heart full of gold and deep in my heart I know all he needs is to understand God's love for him and to accept it. Jesus Christ is his only change agent. Greg grew up broken and hurt and that is why he didn't know how to fully and wholly love me. Hurt people, hurt people and when you have a void in your heart, you often fill it with the wrong things (affairs, anger, etc.). I understand grace more than ever and I pray that I can continue to extend it to others. It does not matter how bad they hurt me; how many times; nor how deep the wounds. I want to continue in grace, extending the same grace God has given and continues to give me. We can't measure sin or compare it. The pain he inflicted on me is no different than the sin I committed towards my own body, to others and most importantly, to God. I am moving forward with life trusting God in every moment.

I am remaining in His love.
Remaining in His Peace.
Remaining in His Rest.

One final thing that remains is **hope**. I am remaining in this hope, meaning I parked my life here. This is the hope that Bailey had in her heart, the hope that gleaned through her eyes and her perfect little dimples. The hope that although life on earth is hard, heaven is easy. No longer do I have to wonder or struggle with the thought of "if I will see her again". Satan caused me to question this for many months after she passed away. I didn't have much hope in this truth because the Bible isn't too clear on this subject. But God restored my hope that I will. He reminded me of the scripture in 2 Samuel 12:23, *"But why should I fast when he is dead? Can I bring him back again? I will go to him one day, but he cannot return to me."* David understood this truth that he would indeed be reunited with his son and I share in this same hope.

When we are faced with the **grief of life and the grief of loss** we have two options: we can become bitter or we can trust in God's ultimate plan and become better. I have chosen the latter. Every day I trust the process of better and I am seeing the fruit of it all. God is faithful!

It's hard for me to believe that Bailey would have been three this year. It's crazy how time doesn't stop even when life does, by way of death. In the early stages of grief, you cry because you feel as though you can't go on without your child but as the years pass, those tears turn into "I can't believe I have continued to live without you". Just thinking how many days and nights have passed is astonishing to me. Again, God is faithful and if He has carried me through the roughest season of my life, surely, He will do the same for you.

Life starts and Ends with Gods love

When you understand this, then you'll understand that God's love for you doesn't shift when death occurs. Life has a way of shifting, people change but God's love for you never does. His unconditional love for His children is anchored deep in the beginning of creation. He created you because of this profound love, and during the days when you feel overwhelmed and burdened, remember that His love is there to sustain and carry you. Keep holding on, keep trusting and keep relying on God's unfailing love. People fail us. Our employers fail us. Marriages fail. Friendships fail. Business deals fail. Life fails us. Death fails us. But God's love, is eternally unfailing. So, there it is, not even grief can separate you from the love of Christ.

As long as we are on earth we will experience hurt. We will continue to require and rely on God's healing and His grace to get through these times. I admonish you to love your enemies, forgive as often as needed and Trust God with your grief from life and grief from loss. Always allow your love to remain for God and towards others. This is the Lord's greatest command.

Love-Bettye Nicole

Who shall separate us from the love of Christ? shall tribulation, or distress, or persecution, or famine, or nakedness, or peril, or sword
As it is written, For thy sake we are killed all the day long; we are accounted as sheep for the slaughter. Nay, in all these things we are more than conquerors through him that loved us.
For I am persuaded, that neither death, nor life, nor angels, nor principalities, nor powers, nor things present, nor things to come, Nor height, nor depth, nor any other creature, shall be able to separate us from the love of God, which is in Christ Jesus our Lord. Romans 8:35-39 KJV

O death, where is thy sting? O grave, where is thy victory? 1Corinthians 15:55 KJV

www.ingramcontent.com/pod-product-compliance
Lightning Source LLC
Chambersburg PA
CBHW051841090426
42736CB00011B/1915